The Tech Audible

The Tech Audible

A Playbook for Entering the Tech Field

Chase Minnifield

BEP
BUSINESS EXPERT PRESS
Leader in applied, concise business books

First published in 2025 by
Business Expert Press, LLC
222 East 46th Street, New York, NY 10017
www.businessexpertpress.com

ISBN-13: 978-1-63742-794-1 (paperback)
ISBN-13: 978-1-63742-795-8 (ebook)

Business Expert Press Entrepreneurship and Small Business Management Collection

First edition: 2025

10 9 8 7 6 5 4 3 2 1

EU SAFETY REPRESENTATIVE
Mare Nostrum Group B.V.
Mauritskade 21D
1091 GC Amsterdam
The Netherlands
gpsr@mare-nostrum.co.uk

I dedicate this book to my grandmother, Catherine Minnifield, better known to me as my Granny. My Granny was a guiding light in my life, raising me alongside my parents and always being there with her unwavering love and support. She meant the world to me, and her influence is something I carry with me every day.

Granny passed on April 9th, 2024, a couple of months before I decided to write this book, but her words continue to resonate with me. I remember sitting with her at her house, talking about life, and she would always say, "I was watching your football game on TV, and you can't be letting those people push you around like that—you got to 'Get 'em'." I'd laugh, but Granny was serious. No matter how big, how smart, or how fast, we compete and fight for what's ours.

Her spirit of determination and strength is something I cherish deeply. I apply that same energy long after my football days are over, and no matter what room I walk into, I belong there—and I make sure we "Get 'em." Thank you, Granny, for instilling that in me. This book is for you, and I will always carry that spirit of knowing we can do all things. I love you.

Description

Call the Audible and Lead Your Business into the Future!

Are you ready to transform your business into a tech-driven powerhouse? Whether you're launching a new tech company or looking to leverage technology to grow your existing business, *The Tech Audible* delivers clear, actionable strategies to help you succeed.

Chase Minnifield—former NFL player and Forbes 30 Under 30 tech entrepreneur—shares the proven methods that helped him go from professional athlete to successful tech founder. This playbook simplifies the world of technology and equips you with step-by-step guidance to:

- **Quickly transition your business into a thriving tech venture**
- **Create technology solutions** that unlock new revenue streams
- **Secure funding** and build a team that drives innovation
- **Overcome obstacles** and scale your business with confidence

Packed with real-world examples and practical insights, *The Tech Audible* is designed for entrepreneurs at any level, even those new to tech. No matter your starting point, this book will help you start a tech company.

Contents

Foreword

My journey from Lexington, Kentucky, as an athlete to becoming a tech entrepreneur has been extraordinary and filled with invaluable lessons. I'm Chase Minnifield, a former defensive back for the Washington Redskins, and a four-time entrepreneur honored to be inducted into Forbes' 2019 class of 30 under 30. Today, I serve as the CEO and founder of EZOS, formerly known as EZTurn, a property management autopilot software designed to automate property maintenance scheduling workflows for optimal team and property success. With over 300K users on our platform, EZOS, short for Easy Operations, is a venture-backed tech company that has made significant strides in the property management industry.

My entrepreneurial journey began at the age of 25, shortly after my NFL career ended. My first company, Helping Hand, a limited liability company (LLC), was established to provide moving, cleaning, and apartment turnover services for college dormitories and student housing complexes. Since its inception, Helping Hand has expanded its services nationwide, partnering with numerous universities. Recently, we pivoted our business model to focus on security guard services, evolving into a franchise where I award franchisees around the country with Helping Hands businesses. This venture has not only generated over $15M in revenue but also created thousands of jobs nationwide. Through Helping Hand, I am committed to championing minority entrepreneurship by offering franchises for free or at a discount to people of color and providing the necessary resources and one-on-one coaching to help them scale, sustain, and grow their businesses under the Helping Hand umbrella.

In addition to Helping Hand, I am the founder of Gard Technologies, a company that leverages artificial intelligence (AI) to revolutionize public safety. Our two apps, Gard and GardX, are up and coming game-changers for the security industry. Gard optimizes security operations from hiring to monitoring, incorporating AI for reporting and geofencing, while GardX enhances public safety by routing users along the safest paths using real-time data from nearby security guards. Together, these products enhance security efficiency and public safety, showcasing the transformative power of technology and also me utilizing my industry knowledge to then advance the industry.

My passion for giving back extends beyond my business ventures. I am also the founder of the Minnifield Foundation, a nonprofit organization dedicated to empowering and inspiring underserved youth through arts, academics, and athletics. This foundation is a testament to my belief in the potential of every young individual and my commitment to creating opportunities for them to thrive.

I hold an MA in Sports Administration from the University of Louisville and a BS in Sociology from the University of Virginia. These academic experiences have shaped my approach to business and leadership, providing me with a solid foundation to navigate the challenges of entrepreneurship. Writing this book has been a reflection on my journey from traditional business operations to embracing technology and innovation. My aim is to share the insights and lessons I've learned along the way, guiding other entrepreneurs in transforming their small businesses knowledge into new tech companies. This book is a culmination of my experiences, successes, and failures, offering a roadmap for those looking to get into tech.

Transitioning from a professional athlete to an entrepreneur was a monumental shift, but the discipline, teamwork, and perseverance I developed in sports became invaluable assets in the business world. As an NFL player, I was accustomed to a regimented schedule, intense physical training, and the constant pursuit of excellence. These experiences taught me the importance of resilience, a quality that proved essential when I faced the inevitable challenges of starting and growing a business.

After retiring from the NFL, I was determined to find a new path that would allow me to make a meaningful impact. The idea of creating Helping Hand, LLC, stemmed from my own experiences as a student-athlete. I recognized a significant need for reliable moving, cleaning, and turnover services in college dormitories and student housing complexes. The transition from sports to business was not easy, but I was driven by the same competitive spirit and commitment to success that had fueled my athletic career.

The early days of Helping Hand, LLC, were filled with hard work, long hours, and a steep learning curve. I quickly realized that running a business required a different set of skills than playing football. I had to learn about operations, marketing, customer service, and financial management. Despite the challenges, the experience was incredibly rewarding. Seeing the positive impact we had on the lives of students and universities was a source of great pride.

As Helping Hand, LLC, grew, we began to expand our services and reach. We partnered with numerous universities across the country, providing essential services that made a difference in the lives of thousands of students. This expansion brought new challenges and opportunities. Managing a growing team, ensuring consistent service quality, and maintaining strong relationships with our clients were all critical to our success.

Recognizing the need to adapt and innovate, we decided to pivot our business model to focus on security guard services. This shift was driven by a desire to address another significant need in the market and to leverage our existing relationships and expertise. Transforming Helping Hand, LLC, into a franchise model allowed us to expand our reach even further, providing opportunities for aspiring entrepreneurs across the country. One of the most fulfilling aspects of this venture has been our commitment to championing minority entrepreneurship. By offering franchises for free or even at a discount to people of color, we are not only creating jobs but also empowering individuals to build and grow their own businesses. The success stories of our franchisees are a testament to the power of opportunity and support. Seeing them thrive and contribute to their communities has been incredibly rewarding.

The differentiator for Helping Hand, LLC, and for our franchisees is our access and use of Gard. In order to give our company an advantage, we needed to create a new software based on our experiences and the gaps we saw in the industry. The ideas behind Gard Technologies came from a deep understanding of the challenges faced by security companies today and the potential for technology to transform this sector. Gard Technologies leverages AI to optimize security operations from hiring and training to monitoring and reporting. Our products, Gard and GardX, have not only new standards for efficiency and safety in the industry but also give our clients a better experience when working with security companies.

Gard Technologies represents the culmination of my experiences and insights gained from running Helping Hand, LLC, and is exactly what I did with EZOS and am showing you how to do in this book.

The decision to transition from traditional business operations to embracing technology and innovation was driven by a desire to stay ahead of the curve and address emerging market needs. Technology has the power to transform industries, streamline operations, and create new opportunities for growth. By leveraging technology, we have been able to enhance the value we provide to our customers and stay competitive in a rapidly evolving landscape.

EZOS, formerly known as EZTurn, is a prime example of how technology can revolutionize traditional business models. Initially focused on student housing turn software, EZOS has evolved into a comprehensive property management autopilot software. The platform's ability to streamline operations, improve efficiency, and enhance communication has made it an invaluable tool for property managers and teams. Our commitment to continuous improvement and innovation has been key to our success.

Writing this book has been a reflective and rewarding experience. It has allowed me to take a step back and examine the journey that has brought me to this point. The lessons I've learned, the challenges I've overcome, and the successes I've achieved are all part of the story I want to share with aspiring entrepreneurs. My goal is to provide a roadmap for those looking to transform their small businesses into tech-driven solutions and to not make getting into tech seem so daunting. This book is not just a recounting of my experiences but also a practical guide filled with actionable insights and strategies. From identifying market needs and leveraging technology to building a strong team and scaling your business, the chapters ahead cover the critical aspects of launching and sustaining a successful tech company. Each chapter is designed to provide you with the knowledge and tools you need to navigate your entrepreneurial journey with confidence.

One of the key lessons I've learned throughout my journey is the importance of resilience and adaptability. Entrepreneurship is filled with uncertainties and challenges, and the ability to adapt and persevere is crucial to long-term success. There have been times when things didn't go as planned, when setbacks seemed insurmountable, and when the future was uncertain. During these times, resilience and adaptability have been my guiding principles. For example, the pivot from providing moving and cleaning services to focusing on security guard services was a significant shift that required a new strategy and approach. Similarly, transitioning from a traditional business model to a tech-driven one involved embracing new technologies and methodologies. Each of these transitions came with its own set of challenges, but they also presented opportunities for growth, change, and innovation.

Another critical factor in my success has been building a strong and dedicated team. No entrepreneur can achieve success alone; it takes a team of talented and committed individuals to bring a vision to life. At Helping Hand, LLC, Gard Technologies, and EZOS, I have been fortunate to work with exceptional people who share my passion and dedication. Building a strong team involves not only hiring the right people but also fostering a culture of collaboration, innovation, and mutual support. Empowering team members, providing opportunities for professional growth, and recognizing their contributions have been key to maintaining a motivated and high-performing team. Creating an environment where everyone feels valued and inspired to do their best work is essential for achieving collective success.

As I look ahead, I am excited about the future and the opportunities that lie ahead. The landscape of entrepreneurship and technology is constantly evolving, and staying ahead requires continuous learning, innovation, and a willingness to adapt. I am committed to continuing to push the boundaries, explore new possibilities, and create solutions that make a positive impact. The journey from athlete to entrepreneur has been filled with challenges, triumphs, and invaluable lessons. Each step has shaped who I am today and has fueled my passion for entrepreneurship and innovation. Writing this book is a way to share that journey, to inspire others, and to provide practical guidance for those looking to embark on their own entrepreneurial paths.

The Tech Audible is a blueprint for transformation to the next level. The steps to take your small business into a thriving tech company. It contains the tools, insights, and strategies you need to navigate the entrepreneurial landscape and achieve your dreams. Whether you are just starting out or looking to scale your existing business, this book will provide you with the knowledge and inspiration to succeed. So let's embark on this journey together. Welcome to a world where your vision can become a reality, where your hard work and dedication can create something extraordinary. This book will change your life, and I am honored to be a part of your entrepreneurial journey. Let's get started!

PART 1

Laying the Foundation

CHAPTER 1

The Birth of an Idea

Every success story begins with a strong foundation. Whether you're building a championship-winning sports team or transforming a small business into a tech company that disrupts an industry, the principles are the same: a solid foundation allows you to push forward with confidence when challenges arise. But in today's rapidly evolving world, the foundation of a thriving business is increasingly intertwined with technology.

Why tech? Because the opportunity is unprecedented. In nearly every industry, tech is driving innovation, changing how business is done, and creating wealth on a massive scale. The people who are best positioned to take advantage of this shift aren't the tech gurus or Silicon Valley elites; they are the business owners, entrepreneurs, and professionals who know their industries inside and out. You, as a small business owner, already have the expertise. Now, imagine pairing that knowledge with tech to create solutions that not only transform your business but also potentially revolutionize your industry.

For many, the hesitation to dive into the tech world comes from a lack of technical knowledge. That hesitation is costing potential innovators millions, if not billions, in revenue. The truth is, you don't need to be a tech expert to start a tech company—you just need to understand your industry's pain points better than anyone else. The rest can be learned or delegated. What you do need is the willingness to see beyond your current business model and identify how technology can scale what you're already doing—faster, smarter, and more profitably.

Consider this: If you, as a small business owner, don't leverage your expertise to develop tech solutions in your field, someone else will. And they may have far less understanding of the actual needs, frustrations, and opportunities within your industry. Who better to solve the most pressing issues in your industry than you? By sitting on your experience and not acting, you could be leaving millions, if not billions, of dollars on the table—money that's just waiting to be made by the person who understands the problem well enough to create the right solution.

This is where I was when I first started my journey from athlete to tech entrepreneur. When I transitioned from my career in the NFL to running my business, I didn't have a tech background. But I knew my industry's pain points because I lived them every day. It became clear to me that my frustrations were my opportunities—the same is true for you.

The first step in transforming a small business into a tech company begins with understanding this simple truth: your frustrations are your blueprint. The obstacles and inefficiencies you experience in your business today are the foundation of the tech solution you could create tomorrow. You don't need to look far to find a problem worth solving—often, the best tech innovations stem from the everyday struggles that make running your business harder than it should be.

When I founded my first tech company, EZTurn (now EZOS), the problem I wanted to solve was right in front of me. I was working in student housing management and encountered the same issues year after year during the turnover season. Property managers had no real-time way of tracking our progress, leading to inefficiencies. Every morning, I'd get calls from managers asking, "How's it going?"—a question that revealed the lack of transparency in the system. And invoicing? That was another nightmare. As my business grew and expanded into multiple locations, keeping track of completed work and the invoicing process became a logistical challenge that only multiplied over time.

It didn't take long for me to realize that these frustrations were not just my problem—they were industrywide. That's when I had my lightbulb moment: if I was facing these challenges, surely others were too. This insight led to the creation of EZTurn, a platform designed to give property managers real-time updates and streamline invoicing for vendors. What began as a solution to my own problems, quickly became a tool that transformed how property management teams operate. And that's the power of combining industry expertise with tech innovation.

Take a moment to reflect on your business. Where are the inefficiencies, the frustrations, and the bottlenecks? What causes delays, increases costs, or leads to headaches for you or your customers? These aren't just problems—they are opportunities for innovation. As a business owner, you have a front-row seat to the pain points that need solving, and your industry knowledge is the key to developing the tech solutions that can revolutionize how business is done.

If you don't capitalize on your expertise to develop the tech solutions your industry needs, someone else will. They may have the coding skills, but without your deep knowledge of the industry, they'll lack the critical insight needed to solve the problem effectively. That's why the best people to create these new tech companies and lead industry change are those who know the industry best—you.

Identifying your pain points is only the beginning. The next step is critical: validating that these problems are worth solving. In my case, the need for real-time updates and simplified invoicing wasn't just a problem I faced—it was a widespread issue within the property management industry. This realization was the turning point where frustration transformed into opportunity.

To validate your problem, reach out to your customers, your clients, or your peers. Ask them pointed questions: Do they experience the same issues? Would they value a solution to these problems? These conversations are invaluable—they ensure that you're not developing a product based on assumptions, but rather on real, verified needs.

Market research is equally important. You need to understand the landscape you're entering. Are there existing solutions that aim to solve similar problems? If so, what are their strengths, and more importantly, their weaknesses? Your goal is to find the gaps—those overlooked areas where your solution can shine.

Who are you building this solution for? This question is not merely academic; it's fundamental. Knowing exactly who your target users are will help you refine your product and tailor your message. For EZOS, the answer was clear: property managers and vendors. They were the ones feeling the pain, and by understanding their specific needs, I was able to develop a product that served them well.

And don't forget to analyze the market itself—its size, its potential for growth. These insights will not only guide your development process but will also be critical when you start speaking with investors. A validated market is a market worth entering.

Now comes the most exhilarating part: building the solution. This is where the foundation you've laid—understanding the pain points and validating the need—begins to pay off. But here's the truth: building the solution isn't just about writing code or developing a product. It's about delivering value. And value comes from solving the right problem in the simplest, most effective way possible.

The key here is focus. Develop a minimum viable product (MVP). An MVP is a stripped-down version of your solution that addresses the core pain points without any unnecessary bells and whistles. When I started EZTurn, I didn't try to build an all-encompassing system from day one. I honed in on two key features: real-time updates for property managers and streamlined invoicing for vendors. These were the pain points that mattered most, and solving them created immediate value.

Simplicity is your ally. The narrower your initial focus, the faster you can get your product into the hands of users. And here's the truth: your users will teach you what comes next. They will show you what works, what doesn't, and what they need more of. The beauty of an MVP is that it gets you to that crucial feedback loop faster. Once it's out there, the real learning begins.

Your first version won't be perfect—it's not supposed to be. What matters is how you respond to feedback. Every interaction with a user is an opportunity to refine, enhance, and evolve. When I launched the initial version of EZTurn, feedback came pouring in. Some property managers wanted additional reporting features, others suggested more customization options. But rather than try to implement every suggestion, I stayed true to the product's core mission: transparency and simplicity. By doing so, I was able to improve the product without losing sight of its original purpose.

It's important to acknowledge that no one builds a tech company alone. Surround yourself with people who have complementary skills—developers who can execute your vision, designers who can ensure your product is intuitive, and strategists who can help scale the business. Assembling the right team is as important as building the right product.

At EZTurn, I worked with developers who brought my ideas to life. Their technical expertise filled in the gaps where my knowledge fell short, and together, we created something far more impactful than I could have built alone. Collaboration isn't just valuable—it's essential.

Once your solution is in the hands of users, and feedback is helping you refine it, start thinking about scale. Growth is the natural next step, but it must be guided by data and user needs. As EZTurn gained traction, I realized that its core features could benefit other segments of the property management industry, not just student housing. This expansion was deliberate, based on market demand and a clear growth strategy.

So, what action can you take today? First, identify pain points: take a deep dive into your business operations and list at least three frustrations or inefficiencies that slow you down. Second, validate the problem: talk to five customers or clients to confirm that they share these frustrations and would be willing to pay for a solution. Third, conduct market research: analyze existing solutions, identify gaps, and define your target market with clarity. Fourth, develop an MVP: build a simple, focused version of your product that solves the most pressing pain points. Finally, gather feedback: launch your MVP, gather input from real users, and iterate based on their feedback.

The foundation of any successful tech company is built on understanding real problems, validating them, and then delivering a solution that meets the needs of your target market. What starts as frustration can become the spark of innovation. Your business is poised for transformation—this is where the journey begins.

CHAPTER 2

Would You Be Your Own Customer?

Starting a tech company based on your expertise requires more than just identifying a problem—it demands a thorough evaluation of whether you would actually use the solution you're building. In this chapter, we explore how you can assess your product from a customer's perspective. This process is essential because if the product doesn't solve a significant problem for you, it's unlikely to do so for others.

Why Start With Yourself?

As a small business owner, you have a unique vantage point—first-hand experience of the pain points in your industry. Many great tech companies are born out of the founder's frustration with existing solutions. Consider this: would you be willing to pay for your own product? If your answer is yes, then you've already validated one key aspect of your business idea.

For instance, let's look at Uber. The founders of Uber created the company because they had a personal frustration and also seen this frustration in real time with getting cabs to the airport, or for any other functions. They found a way to solve their own problems that many other people could have thought of because they experienced it as well, but they acted on it and created a billion dollar company and one of the greatest start-ups in the tech era.

When I was working in property management, the inefficiencies in tracking vendor progress during turnover seasons were driving me crazy. That frustration became the foundation of EZOS. I was solving my own problem, which gave me confidence that others in the industry would also benefit from the solution. Much like Houston's journey with

Dropbox, solving a personal frustration can be a powerful motivator and a great validator of your product's potential.

The First Step: Self-Assessment

The self-assessment begins by honestly evaluating whether your product would solve a critical problem in your business. Ask yourself:

- Does this solution address a pain point I experience regularly?
- Would this solution save me time or money?
- How would this solution improve my day-to-day operations?

For example, with EZOS, I knew that automating progress tracking and invoicing would save me hours of administrative work and reduce the stress of managing multiple vendors. This realization gave me confidence that other property managers would see the same value.

Self-assessment is a critical step for any entrepreneur. It helps ensure that your solution addresses a real need, rather than being a product of your imagination. Often, the most successful tech solutions are those that directly address frustrations the founder has personally encountered. Steve Jobs, for example, famously believed in creating products that he would want to use himself, which led to the creation of some of the most iconic devices of our time. But simply solving your own problem isn't enough—you need to make sure that this problem is shared by others.

Expanding Your Perspective

While your self-assessment is valuable, it's also limited by your individual experience. What if your problem is too niche? This is where you need to start looking beyond your own situation. Begin by discussing your solution with peers in your industry. Ask them if they experience the same frustrations and how they currently solve them. You'll be surprised at how much insight you can gain by simply asking others who are in the same boat.

A good example of this process comes from Slack. Stewart Butterfield originally developed Slack as an internal communication tool for his team while working on a different project. After realizing how much it improved team collaboration, he shared it with other companies and found that they faced similar communication issues. This broader validation helped turn Slack into one of the most popular business communication platforms today.

Developing Customer Personas

Once you're certain that you would be your own customer, the next step is to identify who else would benefit from your solution. Creating customer personas helps you move beyond your own experience and understand the wider market.

Customer personas are fictional representations of your ideal customers, based on real data. For EZOS, I created personas for both property managers and vendors, as they represented the core users of the software. By understanding their specific needs and pain points, I was able to tailor the product to better serve them.

To create accurate personas, consider the following:

- **Demographics**: Age, gender, location, occupation.
- **Goals**: What do they hope to achieve by using your product?
- **Challenges**: What are their most pressing pain points?
- **Buying Behavior**: How do they make purchasing decisions?

Building detailed customer personas can help you focus on what matters most to your users, ensuring that your product development aligns with their needs. This also helps to avoid the common pitfall of designing a product that is too tailored to your own needs, rather than the needs of a broader audience.

Avoiding the Trap of Self-Bias

One potential pitfall in building a tech solution for yourself is self-bias. While your experience provides valuable insight, you must ensure that your product isn't overly tailored to your unique needs at the expense of the wider market. This is why customer personas are essential—they allow you to see your product through the eyes of others and prevent you from falling into the trap of designing a product that only serves a small segment of users.

A good way to counteract this is by gathering feedback early and often from people outside your immediate circle. As you move into the development phase, start sharing prototypes or mockups with potential users to see how they react. Their feedback can help you identify blind spots and make necessary adjustments to appeal to a larger audience.

Transitioning to Broader Validation

At this stage, you've answered a critical question: would you use your own product? But your idea's success doesn't rest solely on your validation. It's now time to expand the scope and gather feedback from potential customers, which will allow you to refine your solution further.

This is where the next step comes in—conducting market research and interviewing potential customers. These steps will give you a deeper understanding of whether the product you believe in resonates with others. You've validated your idea on a personal level, but now you need to validate it with a broader audience. The next chapter will guide you through this process, showing you how to conduct effective customer interviews that reveal whether your solution truly solves a widespread problem.

Conclusion

Self-assessment is a powerful tool in the early stages of developing a tech solution. By asking whether you would be your own customer, you can gain valuable insight into your product's potential. However, to truly validate your idea, you need to go beyond your personal experience and understand the needs of the broader market. As you move forward, the focus shifts to engaging with potential customers, listening to their feedback, and refining your product to meet their needs. That's where the real journey begins.

CHAPTER 3

Interviewing Potential Customers

Market research is crucial for understanding whether your idea holds value beyond your own belief. In my case, I was fairly certain that the solutions I was building would be valuable, whether or not others in the industry saw their potential immediately. My perspective was that it was a win–win: either it would become a widely adopted tech solution, or it would significantly streamline and improve my own business operations, leading to better margins and fewer headaches. The importance of market research is clear, as it has been ingrained in me from sports my entire life. A quick example of this from sports is watching film of our opponents, something I had been doing since little league football as a seven-year old. I would watch film for hours and hours, looking for tendencies from teams and players to have the best understanding and knowledge of my opponent and how I would approach the game strategically. The strategy I would come up with was "my plan," and it was derived from my "market research." I had full confidence in my plan after conducting the market research, and because of that, I would perform better. The same applies in business: the more market research and feedback you get, the more confidence you gain, and the better you will perform.

With EZOS, even though I was confident in the value of my idea, I knew I needed to validate it with others to continue to increase my confidence. My market research wasn't extensive at first; I casually asked peers in the industry about their thoughts over coffee or lunch. These informal conversations provided initial insights but lacked depth. The real breakthrough came when I started drawing out wireframes and creating a "fake app." This technique allowed for more productive conversations and provided a visual representation of the vision in my head. Sometimes, explaining something that doesn't exist yet can feel like speaking another language, no matter how good you are at communicating. A visual aid can bridge that gap.

Another important lesson is that not everyone will understand or support your vision. People might dismiss your idea as dumb, stupid, or a waste of time. Remember, the vision was given to you for a reason. Don't let naysayers discourage you. Instead, focus on the feedback from those who see the potential and share your enthusiasm. These are the people who might become your cofounders.

For instance, during a market research lunch, I shared my vision for EZOS with Lincoln. He found the idea intriguing and believed in it as much as I did. This initial conversation led to a partnership, and we have been building the company together since 2018.

The first step in interviewing potential customers is preparation. Clearly outline what you want to achieve with these interviews. Are you trying to validate the need for your solution? Are you seeking feedback on specific features? Once your goals are defined, develop a list of questions that will help you understand your potential customers' pain points, their current solutions, and their willingness to pay for a new solution. Avoid leading questions that could bias their responses.

Next, identify potential interviewees. Reach out to people in your industry who represent your target market. These could be current clients, peers, or even individuals you meet at industry events. When conducting the interviews, ensure that the interviewee feels at ease. This can be over a casual coffee or lunch, or a formal meeting if appropriate. Focus on listening more than talking. Your goal is to gather insights, not to sell your idea at this stage. If possible, use wireframes or prototypes to help convey your idea. This makes it easier for others to understand and provide meaningful feedback.

After conducting the interviews, it's time to analyze the feedback. Look for patterns in the responses and identify common themes and recurring issues mentioned by different interviewees. This can highlight the most pressing problems and the most valued features. Not all feedback will be equally valuable, so prioritize insights from individuals who are most representative of your target market. Use this feedback to make informed adjustments to your concept. This iterative process will help you develop a more robust solution.

Through these interviews, you might also identify potential cofounders. Look for individuals who are genuinely excited about your idea and see its potential. Identify people whose skills and experiences complement your own, as a cofounder should bring something to the table that you lack. Ensure that potential cofounders are as committed to the vision as you are. Building a company is a long-term endeavor, and you need partners who are in it for the long haul.

In my experience, Lincoln emerged as a cofounder during one of these market research lunches. His enthusiasm and belief in the vision of EZOS matched mine, and we have been working together ever since.

Interviewing potential customers is a critical step in validating your idea and refining your product. Through preparation, active listening, and thoughtful analysis of feedback, you can ensure that your solution meets real needs in the market. Additionally, this process can help you find like-minded individuals who share your vision and can become invaluable partners in your entrepreneurial journey. Remember, your idea might not resonate with everyone, but the support and belief of a few key people can make all the difference.

Market research is not just about validating your idea; it's about understanding the landscape you're entering. This involves not only talking to potential customers but also studying your competitors and the overall market trends. The more information you have, the better equipped you are to make informed decisions about your product and strategy. One of the most valuable things I took away from market research was where other people saw gaps in tech or in their industry as a whole. This information would lead our product road maps.

When I first started EZOS, I knew that having a deep understanding of the property management industry was essential. I needed to know what other solutions were out there, how they were being used, and what gaps existed in the market. This knowledge would help me position EZOS as a unique and valuable solution.

In addition to customer interviews, I spent a lot of time researching online, reading industry reports, and attending industry conferences.

These activities helped me gather a wealth of information that comple-mented the feedback I was getting from potential customers. It also gave me a broader perspective on the industry and helped me identify emerging trends that could impact my product.

One of the key insights I gained from my market research was the importance of real-time updates and transparency in property manage-ment. Property managers were constantly looking for ways to improve communication and efficiency. This insight was crucial in shaping the features of EZOS and making sure it addressed the most pressing needs of our target market.

Another important aspect of market research is understanding the regulatory environment. Depending on your industry, there may be specific regulations that you need to comply with. For example, in the property management industry, there are regulations around data privacy and security that we needed to consider when developing EZOS. Being aware of these regulations from the start helped us design our product in a way that was compliant and avoided potential legal issues down the road.

Once you have gathered all this information, the next step is to synthesize it and use it to refine your product. This is where the iterative process of product development comes into play. Based on the feedback and insights you have gathered, you may need to make changes to your product design, add new features, or even pivot your strategy entirely.

For example, during the development of EZOS, we initially focused on providing a solution for property managers to track turn progress. However, based on the feedback we received from our interviews, we realized that there was also a strong need for better inspection tools and data collection for property managers, tenants, and staff. This led us to add an inspection feature to our product, which became one of the most popular features among our users.

It's important to remember that product development is not a one-time process. Which was something I learned on the journey because initially I thought we would create this product once and let it sell as is and never need to make any more features or fix any problems. This shows how naive I was. EZOS ended up being something we worked on everyday since Day 1. As your business grows and evolves, you will continue to gather feedback from your customers and the market. This ongoing process of listening, learning, and adapting is key to building a successful and sustainable tech company.

In addition to refining your product, market research can also help you develop your marketing and sales strategies. By understanding your target market's needs, preferences, and behaviors, you can tailor your messaging and positioning to resonate with them more effectively. This can help you attract and convert more customers, ultimately driving growth for your business.

For EZOS, our market research revealed that property managers were particularly responsive to case studies and testimonials from other property managers. This insight led us to create a series of case studies that showcased how our product was helping property managers improve their operations. These case studies became a powerful marketing tool and helped us build credibility and trust with our target audience.

Another key finding from our market research was the importance of industry events and conferences. Property managers often attended these events to learn about new solutions and network with their peers. By having a presence at these events, we were able to reach a large number of potential customers and generate interest in our product. This strategy proved to be highly effective in driving awareness and sales for EZOS.

In summary, market research is a critical component of building a successful tech company. It helps you validate your idea, understand your market, refine your product, and develop effective marketing and sales strategies. By taking the time to conduct thorough market research and actively listen to your customers, you can increase your chances of success and build a product that truly meets the needs of your target market.

As you embark on this journey, remember that market research is not a one-time activity. It's an ongoing process that requires continuous effort and attention. Stay curious, keep learning, and be open to feedback. By doing so, you will be better equipped to navigate the challenges of building a tech company and achieve your vision.

One of the most valuable aspects of market research is the opportunity to engage directly with your potential customers and current customers. As CEO, I have found these conversations most valuable at all stages and people love talking to the founders because they can directly provide input that can directly affect their work lives in the future. These conversations can provide a wealth of insights that you may not be able to gather from secondary research alone. They can help you understand the nuances of your customers' pain points, preferences, and behaviors, which can inform your product development and marketing strategies.

During my market research for EZOS, I had the opportunity to speak with dozens of property managers. These conversations were incredibly valuable in helping me understand the day-to-day challenges they faced and how our product could help address those challenges. I learned that property managers were not only looking for a solution to streamline their operations but they also had ideas about a lot of things that need to improve in their day-to-day.

One of the most memorable conversations I had was with a property manager who had been in the industry for over 20 years. She shared with me the frustrations she experienced with the existing property management software and how it often fell short of meeting her needs. She explained that what she really needed was a solution that could provide real-time updates, automate routine tasks, and improve property communication.

This conversation was a turning point for me. It reinforced the importance of listening to your customers and understanding their needs on a deeper level. It also highlighted the value of building a product that not only addresses functional requirements but also enhances the overall user experience.

Based on the feedback I received from these conversations, I made several key changes to the design and functionality of EZOS. For example, we added a feature that allowed property managers to receive automated reports about maintenance updates and other important information. This feature was well-received by our users and became one of the key selling points for our product.

In addition to informing product development, customer interviews can also help you identify potential advocates and early adopters. These individuals can provide valuable testimonials, referrals, and feedback that can help you build momentum and credibility for your product.

For example, one of the property managers I interviewed became an early adopter of EZOS and provided us with a glowing testimonial. She also referred several of her colleagues to our product, which helped us expand our customer base and gain traction in the market.

Building strong relationships with your customers is essential for long-term success. By actively engaging with them, listening to their feedback, and continuously improving your product based on their needs, you can build a loyal customer base that will support your growth and success.

In conclusion, interviewing potential customers is a critical step in validating your idea and refining your product. It provides valuable insights that can help you understand your market, develop a more robust solution, and build strong relationships with your customers. By taking the time to prepare, actively listen, and thoughtfully analyze feedback, you can increase your chances of building a successful and sustainable tech company.

Remember, the journey of building a tech company is not a sprint but a marathon. It requires patience, perseverance, and a willingness to learn and adapt. By staying focused on your customers and continuously seeking their feedback, you can build a product that truly meets their needs and drives long-term success for your business.

As you move forward, keep in mind that your idea might not resonate with everyone, but the support and belief of a few key people can make all the difference. Stay true to your vision, remain open to feedback, and never stop learning. With dedication and hard work, you can turn your idea into a successful tech company that makes a meaningful impact in your industry.

The process of interviewing potential customers and conducting market research is an ongoing journey that will continue to evolve as your business grows. Embrace this journey with curiosity and determination, and you will be well on your way to building a tech company that stands the test of time.

CHAPTER 4

Conducting a SWOT Analysis

I used to think a Strengths, Weaknesses, Opportunities, and Threats (SWOT) analysis was a waste of time until I realized it was exactly how I achieved success in football. Let me explain. In football, although we never called it SWOT, we constantly analyzed our strengths, weaknesses, opportunities, and threats. As a cornerback in college and the NFL, I always knew that my strengths were my jumping ability, quickness, and football IQ. My weaknesses were my physical strength, straight-line speed, and sometimes being overly passionate. I was aware of these factors every snap I played, and they influenced how I positioned myself for the best chance of success.

In football, opportunities meant knowing when to be more aggressive to make game-changing plays based on coverages, game situations, and more. Threats involved understanding potential dangers from coverages, personnel, down and distance, and so on. Recognizing these threats allowed me to adjust my techniques and alignments for better outcomes. Knowing a threat was coming was always preferable to being blindsided by it. This is the essence of a SWOT analysis, applied to the NFL. Once I realized this, I knew I had to apply the same understanding to my business.

When I created EZOS, conducting a SWOT analysis helped me identify the strengths, weaknesses, opportunities, and threats associated with my product. This process provided a clear picture of where EZOS stood and guided the development of a solid business foundation.

A SWOT analysis is a strategic planning tool used to identify the internal and external factors that can impact your business. Strengths are the internal attributes that give your product an advantage over others. For EZOS, the strengths included my deep knowledge and understanding of the property management space. Having worked in this industry, I knew the ins and outs of property management operations, which allowed me to design a product that directly addressed the pain points I had experienced.

Weaknesses are internal factors that might hinder your product's success. One of the significant weaknesses I identified was the uncertainty about whether property managers would pay for this product. It was a brand new idea, and Turn software wasn't a budget line item for any properties I had ever heard of. Additionally, my lack of experience in selling tech solutions posed a challenge in gaining market traction and losing all the money and time I put into this venture.

Opportunities are external factors that your product could exploit to its advantage. For EZOS, the opportunities were substantial. The entire student housing and college markets were potential customers, representing low-hanging fruit. The need for efficiency in property management was high, and there was a clear gap in the market for a solution like EZOS.

Threats are external factors that could jeopardize your product's success. One of the primary threats I identified was the potential for big property management companies to develop similar software. If these large companies decided to create their own Turn management solutions, it could divert interest away from what I was building.

By conducting a SWOT analysis, I gained a comprehensive understanding of where EZOS stood in the market. This analysis allowed me to capitalize on strengths and opportunities while addressing weaknesses and preparing for potential threats.

After completing the SWOT analysis, the next step was to create a Lean Model Canvas. This tool helps entrepreneurs map out the key elements of their business model on a single page, providing a clear and concise overview. The Lean Model Canvas consists of several components:

1. **Problem:** Identify the top three problems your product solves. For EZOS, the main problems were the lack of real-time updates for property managers, the inefficiency of invoicing for ven-

dors and causing properties to be overcharged, and automated progress updates so no one was caught off guard with disappointing results.

2. **Customer Segments:** Define who your target customers are. EZOS's primary customers were property managers and vendors in the student housing market.

3. **Unique Value Proposition:** Describe what makes your product unique and why customers should choose it over competitors. EZOS offered transparency and efficiency, and would save money and time for properties while allowing vendors to get paid quicker, which were not available in existing solutions.

4. **Solution:** Outline how your product solves the identified problems. EZOS provided real-time progress tracking and an easy, fast, and audited way to invoice, addressing the core issues faced by property managers and vendors.

5. **Channels:** Determine the pathways through which you will reach your customers. This included direct sales, industry events, and online marketing.

6. **Revenue Streams:** Identify how your product will generate revenue. For EZOS, potential revenue streams included subscription fees and service charges.

7. **Cost Structure:** List the key costs associated with developing and running your product. This included development costs, marketing expenses, and customer support tools.

8. **Key Metrics:** Define the metrics that will help you measure the success of your product. These could include customer acquisition costs, retention rates, and user engagement levels. For EZOS it was the number of clients, clients satisfaction level, and how much we saved our clients.

9. **Unfair Advantage:** Identify what sets your product apart that cannot be easily copied or bought. For EZOS, it was always a concern of ours that someone would copy our platform, but our advantage was always that we had a deep knowledge and personal experience with what we were building. This ended up

being our greatest asset because EZOS worked for the customer and it solved what the customer needed.

One of the critical components of the Lean Model Canvas is the revenue model. Developing a sustainable revenue model is essential for the long-term success of your tech company. For EZOS, I considered various revenue streams: subscription fees, service charges, and usage-based fees. Charging a monthly or annual subscription fee for access to the software provided a steady and predictable revenue stream. Additional fees for premium features or services, such as custom integrations or priority support, allowed for flexibility and the ability to offer tiered pricing. Charging based on the amount of usage, such as the number of properties managed, number of units, or the volume of invoices generated, aligned with the value provided to the customers. Ultimately we chose a subscription based on usage model, but we didn't start there and it took us a year to figure out the best revenue model.

Choosing the right revenue model depends on understanding your customers' willingness to pay and the value your product offers. It's important to test different models and gather feedback to find the most effective approach. My advice would be to understand how your customer is paying for current technology they are using and try to fit your product into that model.

Conducting a SWOT analysis and creating a Lean Model Canvas are foundational steps in building a successful tech company. By understanding your product's strengths, weaknesses, opportunities, and threats, and mapping out the key elements of your business model, you can develop a solid foundation for your venture. For EZOS, these strategic tools helped guide the development process and ensured that we were addressing real market needs. As you embark on your journey, remember that a strong foundation is critical to achieving long-term success.

In conclusion, the process of conducting a SWOT analysis and developing a Lean Model Canvas was instrumental in the successful creation and growth of EZOS. These strategic tools provided a comprehensive understanding of the market landscape and allowed me to build a product that met real needs and offered unique value. By systematically identifying SWOT, and mapping out a clear business model, I was able to navigate the complexities of the tech industry and establish a strong foundation for my company. As you embark on your own entrepreneurial journey, I encourage you to embrace these tools and invest the time and effort required to lay a solid foundation for your tech venture. The insights and clarity gained from this process will serve as a roadmap, guiding you toward sustainable success and growth.

CHAPTER 5

Leveraging Technology Trends

In today's rapidly evolving technology landscape, staying ahead isn't just an advantage—it's a fundamental necessity. With each new wave of innovation, such as artificial intelligence (AI), the Web, or smartphones, comes a fresh opportunity to build transformative businesses that can redefine entire industries. Some of the recent technology trends include: AI, robotics, and blockchain. And everything isn't going to last, but I believe in AI and how it's going to affect the world we live in. At EZOS, we've experienced firsthand the effect of AI as we pivot to embrace it, understanding that the potential to reshape customer experiences and expectations is enormous. This chapter delves into how AI and other emerging technologies are impacting every industry, and how we're leveraging these advancements to drive growth and innovation at EZOS.

The AI Revolution: Shaping the Tech Landscape

AI is not just a buzzword—it's the engine driving the next wave of technological transformation. In the last decade alone, AI has moved from a theoretical concept to a practical tool that businesses across the globe are leveraging to stay competitive. AI's applications are vast, ranging from enhancing customer service through chatbots to automating complex supply chain processes. For many, AI is quickly becoming the cornerstone of modern business strategy, enabling unprecedented efficiency and innovation.

For industries that rely heavily on data, AI offers a way to unlock new insights and optimize operations in ways that were previously unimaginable. In health care, AI can analyze medical records to predict patient needs; in finance, it can detect fraudulent transactions with greater accuracy than human analysts. The implications of AI are profound, and no industry is immune to its impact.

At its core, AI allows businesses to automate complex processes, derive insights from vast amounts of data, and create more personalized customer interactions. As someone who started EZOS without much knowledge of AI, the realization of its potential has been nothing short of revolutionary. We now see AI not just as a tool but as a transformative force that's reshaping the very foundations of our business.

Building EZOS in the Age of AI

When we launched EZOS, our focus was on solving practical problems in property management. At that time, AI was not part of our roadmap. However, as we grew and the tech landscape evolved, it became clear that AI would be crucial in meeting our customers' growing expectations. The beauty of new technologies like AI is that they open up opportunities for creating something entirely new—unicorn companies that redefine industries.

Initially, our approach at EZOS was rooted in traditional methods. We focused on providing value by streamlining property management processes, ensuring that our clients could manage their properties with greater ease and efficiency. This approach worked well, but as AI began to emerge as a dominant force in the tech world, we realized we had to adapt.

Integrating AI into our operations wasn't just about keeping up with the competition; it was about recognizing the ways AI could revolutionize our business model. For instance, by incorporating AI-driven predictive analytics, we were able to transform our maintenance scheduling. Instead of reacting to issues as they arose, we could now anticipate them, allowing property managers to address potential problems before they became costly emergencies. This proactive approach not only improved efficiency but also significantly enhanced tenant satisfaction.

However, this transition wasn't without its challenges. Like many companies, we had to overcome a steep learning curve. We had to understand AI not just as a technology but as a strategic asset that could redefine our business. This meant investing in new tools, training our team, and, perhaps most importantly, shifting our mindset to embrace a future where AI plays a central role.

Opportunities for Innovation in the AI Era

New technologies, such as the iPhone or the Web in their early days, create fertile ground for innovation. AI is no different—it's the new frontier, offering vast opportunities for those willing to embrace it. The key is to identify where AI can add the most value, whether in product development, customer service, or business operations.

At EZOS, AI has opened up new possibilities in property management. By using AI to analyze data from past maintenance records, we can predict when and where issues are likely to arise, allowing us to proactively address them. This not only saves money but also improves the overall experience for tenants. It's a perfect example of how embracing AI can lead to the development of new features that were previously unimaginable.

But AI's potential goes beyond just operational improvements. It's also about creating entirely new business models. For instance, consider how AI is being used to personalize customer experiences in real time. Companies such as Netflix and Amazon have set the bar high, using AI to recommend products and content tailored to individual preferences. This level of personalization is something that all businesses, including EZOS, need to aspire to as customer expectations continue to rise.

One of the most exciting aspects of working with AI is the potential to explore areas that were previously out of reach. For instance, we've begun experimenting with AI-driven chatbots to handle customer inquiries more efficiently. These bots can answer common questions, guide users through processes, and even handle basic troubleshooting, freeing up our human staff to focus on more complex issues. This not only improves customer service but also reduces operational costs.

Smart Integration of AI

While the potential of AI is vast, integrating it into your business model requires a thoughtful approach. At EZOS, we've adopted a strategy that's both smart and growth-focused. We're not just jumping on the AI bandwagon; we're carefully considering how AI can enhance our existing processes and products.

One of the biggest mistakes companies can make when adopting new technology is to implement it without a clear understanding of how it will fit into their overall strategy. AI is no exception. At EZOS, we've taken the time to evaluate where AI can have the most significant impact. For us, this has meant focusing on areas such as predictive maintenance, customer service automation, and data analysis. I've also implemented a rule that we aren't adding AI in areas of our software, unless it provides transformational value, which can result in more sales and more revenue for the company.

For example, we've been cautious about implementing AI in ways that might overwhelm our customers. Instead, we've focused on areas where AI can make a transformational difference, such as predictive maintenance and customer service automation. This approach ensures that we're leveraging AI to improve our services without losing sight of what our customers value most, which is making their job easier and saving them time.

We've also made sure to keep the human element in our AI integrations. While AI can handle many tasks more efficiently than humans, there are still areas where human judgment and empathy are irreplaceable. By combining AI's strengths with human insights, we've been able to create a more balanced approach that enhances our service without sacrificing the personal touch that our customers appreciate, which is the ability to edit/adjust the decisions made by AI if need be.

The Future: AI and Beyond

As we look to the future, it's clear that AI will continue to play a significant role in shaping the tech landscape. But it's not the only emerging technology worth paying attention to. Blockchain, robotics, and other advancements are also set to have a profound impact on how businesses operate.

For example, blockchain technology, which offers unprecedented transparency and security, is something we're keeping a close eye on. While it's not yet a central part of our strategy at EZOS, we see its potential for creating secure, immutable records of transactions and agreements. This could be particularly valuable in property management, where trust and transparency are crucial.

Robotics is another area with exciting possibilities. Imagine a future where routine maintenance tasks are handled by robots, freeing up human workers to focus on more complex issues. While this technology is still in its early stages, we're exploring how it might be integrated into our operations in the future.

However, the most important lesson we've learned at EZOS is that technology should always serve a purpose. It's not about adopting the latest trends for the sake of it; it's about using technology to solve real problems and create value for your customers. With AI, we've found new ways to enhance our product and improve the user experience, and we'll continue to explore how other technologies can contribute to our growth.

The Role of Leadership in Navigating AI Integration

Integrating AI and other emerging technologies into your business isn't just about having the right tools; it's also about leadership. As a leader, you need to be the driving force behind your company's adoption of new technologies. This means staying informed about the latest trends, understanding how they can be applied to your business, and inspiring your team to embrace change. Change and adaptability is important in building a business and staying around through all the competition, which I call competitive stamina.

At EZOS, I've found that leading by example is crucial. When our team sees that I'm committed to learning about AI and exploring its potential, they're more likely to do the same. It's also important to foster a culture of experimentation. Encourage your team to try new things, even if they're outside the scope of your current operations. You never know where the next big breakthrough will come from.

Leadership also means being able to make tough decisions. Not every AI implementation will be successful, and it's important to know when to pivot. At EZOS, we've had to learn from our mistakes and adjust our strategy as we go. This willingness to adapt has been key to our success in integrating AI into our business.

Networking and Collaboration in the AI Era

One of the most valuable lessons I've learned is the importance of networking and collaboration in the tech industry, especially when it comes to AI. No company operates in a vacuum, and staying connected with other tech professionals and businesses is essential for staying ahead of the curve.

Engaging with other tech professionals and businesses can provide new insights and ideas that inform your product development. Collaborations can lead to innovative solutions and shared resources. For example, partnering with a company specializing in blockchain technology could integrate advanced security features into your product without developing them from scratch.

At EZOS, we've made a concerted effort to build relationships with other companies that are also exploring AI. These partnerships have allowed us to share knowledge, pool resources, and even co-brainstorm new solutions. By working together, we're able to achieve more than we could on our own.

Networking also provides an opportunity to learn from others' successes and failures. By attending industry conferences, participating in webinars, and engaging in online communities, we've gained valuable insights into how other companies are leveraging AI. These interactions have helped us refine our strategy and avoid common pitfalls.

Encouraging a Culture of Experimentation

Encouraging a culture of experimentation within your team is another important strategy. Allow room for testing new ideas and technologies, even if they seem outside the immediate scope of your product. This experimentation can lead to unexpected breakthroughs. For example, a side project exploring the use of AI in customer service could result in new features that enhance the user experience and differentiate your product from competitors. As a CEO, you can get caught up in looking forward all the time and focusing on what your team needs to do next that you forget to allow for consistent exploration. Exploration is what your company was founded on and allowing your team to keep exploring that muscle improves team morale.

At EZOS, we've seen firsthand how a willingness to experiment can lead to innovation and increased team morale. For example, our initial attempts at integrating AI were focused on operational efficiencies. However, as we explored different applications of AI, we discovered that it could also be used to enhance our customer service. By experimenting with AI-driven decision making, we were able to create a new automated ticket generation that not only improved customer satisfaction but also saved time and generated more data.

But experimentation doesn't just happen on its own—it needs to be encouraged. As a leader, it's important to create an environment where your team feels safe to try new things, even if they don't always work out. At EZOS, we've made it clear that failure is a part of the process. By fostering a culture where experimentation is valued and expected, we've been able to drive innovation and stay ahead of the competition.

Customer Feedback and Market Needs

Finally, keep a close eye on customer feedback and market needs. Technology should always enhance the user experience and solve their problems. Regularly engaging with your customers to understand their evolving needs and how technology can meet those needs is crucial. This customer-centric approach ensures your product remains relevant and valuable as market conditions change.

At EZOS, we've made customer feedback a central part of our AI strategy. By regularly engaging with our customers, we've been able to identify the areas where AI can make the most significant impact. For example, our customers told us that maintenance issues were one of their biggest pain points. By focusing our AI efforts on predictive maintenance, we've been able to address this need directly, improving customer satisfaction and retention.

But customer needs are always evolving, and it's important to stay adaptable. As new technologies emerge and customer expectations shift, we need to be ready to adjust our strategy. This means staying informed about the latest trends and being willing to pivot when necessary.

Balancing Technology and Business Operations

Balancing the use of advanced technologies in your business operations and integrating them into your product roadmap creates a tech company that is agile, innovative, and responsive to customer needs. Leveraging technology trends effectively means staying informed and adaptable, continuously learning and experimenting, and always keeping the customer at the center of your innovation efforts.

At EZOS, we've learned that technology should never be an end in itself. It's a means to an end—a way to create value for our customers and stay competitive in a rapidly changing market. By balancing the integration of AI with a strong focus on customer needs, we've been able to build a company that's not only innovative but also grounded in real-world value.

Conclusion: Embracing Technology With Purpose

The tech industry is constantly evolving, and staying ahead means being open to new ideas and willing to adapt. At EZOS, we've embraced AI not because it's trendy, but because it aligns with our mission to provide the best possible service to our customers. As you build your tech company, remember that technology is a tool, not a goal. Use it to solve problems, create value, and ultimately, to build something that stands the test of time.

AI and other emerging technologies offer unprecedented opportunities for innovation and growth. By integrating these technologies thoughtfully and strategically, you can create a business that not only survives but also thrives in the ever-changing tech landscape. Stay curious, stay informed, and never stop experimenting. The future of your company depends on your ability to harness the power of technology and turn it into meaningful solutions for your customers.

PART 2

From Concept to Prototype

CHAPTER 6

Wireframing and Prototyping

When I was developing EZOS, my mind was brimming with ideas. I knew I needed to get them down on paper to make sense of them and communicate them effectively. At that time, I had no formal training in app development or technical design. The only thing I knew was drawing plays and coverages and putting together a playbook from my time playing football, so I did exactly that. I printed off hundreds of blank iPad screens and started sketching out how I envisioned the app working. I spread all these screens out on the floor to visualize the user experience. This method, although primitive, helped me understand the flow and functionality of the app from a user's perspective. Little did I know, this process is known as wireframing, and there are far more efficient ways to go about it. Ultimately, I created my tech playbook and utilized this to get my vision on paper and from paper I got it to people who could create it, but just like in football everything happens around the playbook and the more you know the playbook the better you play, in tech the more detailed your wireframes the less issues you will have when working with your developers and getting your software company off the ground!

I share this story to emphasize that you don't need to be a tech expert to start wireframing your ideas. The key is having a vision and finding a way to present it as clearly and detailed as possible to your developers or development team. The book of drawn-out screens I created eventually turned into a multimillion-dollar company. Just because you don't know all the technical jargon doesn't mean you should stop. We'll figure out the details as we go along.

Wireframing is a crucial step in transforming your idea into a functional product. It involves creating a visual guide that represents the skeletal framework of your app or website. Today, there are numerous tools available that make wireframing much easier and more efficient than sketching on paper. Tools such as Figma, Sketch, Adobe XD, and Canva offer a range of features to help you create detailed wireframes quickly.

Leveraging Wireframing Tools

Figma is a web-based design tool that allows real-time collaboration. It's great for wireframing because it offers a wide range of design elements and templates that can help you create detailed wireframes quickly. **Sketch** is a vector graphics editor primarily used for creating user interfaces (UI) and enhancing user experiences (UX) through visual visual designs. It's a powerful tool for creating wireframes and high-fidelity prototypes. Its intuitive interface makes it easy to use, even for beginners. **Adobe XD** is another excellent tool for wireframing and prototyping. It integrates well with other Adobe products and offers features such as auto-animate and voice prototyping, making it a versatile choice for designers. **Canva** offers a more straightforward, design-ready wireframing experience. It's perfect for taking a template and applying your ideas and getting feedback without getting bogged down in the details.

Creating User Flows

User flows are diagrams that map out the steps a user takes to complete a task within your app. Creating user flows helps you understand the user's journey and ensures that your app is intuitive and user-friendly. Start by identifying the main tasks users will perform in your app. For EZOS, these tasks included logging in, viewing property maintenance schedules, updating task statuses, and generating invoices. For each key task, outline the steps a user will take to complete it. This includes every screen they will interact with and the actions they will take on each screen. Consider different user scenarios and edge cases. What happens if a user encounters an error? How can they navigate back to the main task? Designing for these scenarios ensures a smoother user experience. Use wireframing tools to create a visual representation of the user flow. This helps you see the overall structure and make adjustments as needed.

Designing a Prototype

After wireframing and creating user flows, the next step is to design a prototype. A prototype is a preliminary version of your app that allows you to test and refine your ideas before full-scale development. Convert your initial wireframes into high-fidelity versions that include more detailed design elements, such as colors, fonts, and images. Tools such as Invision, Figma, and Sketch allow you to create interactive prototypes. These tools let you add interactions and transitions, making your prototype feel like a real app. Share your prototype with potential users and gather feedback. Observe how they interact with the prototype and take note of any issues or areas for improvement. Use the feedback to make necessary adjustments. Prototyping is an iterative process, and each round of testing brings you closer to a polished product.

When I moved from paper sketches to digital screens, I used a mix of Adobe and Invision to create a prototype of EZOS. Adobe was used for my designs and Invision was where I added the transitions and made it feel real. This prototype became a powerful tool for sales presentations and pitch meetings, allowing potential clients and investors to experience the vision I had in mind. It transformed abstract ideas into tangible, interactive experiences and played a crucial role in our journey to success.

The Importance of Iteration

The process of wireframing and prototyping is not a one-time task; it is an ongoing part of the product development cycle. As you gather feedback and make improvements, you will need to update your wireframes and prototypes. This iterative approach ensures that your product evolves in response to user needs and technological advancements. It also allows you to stay agile and adapt to changes in the market.

Collaborating With Your Development Team

In addition to testing with users, it is also important to involve your development team in the wireframing and prototyping process. Developers can provide valuable insights into the feasibility of your designs and help identify potential technical challenges. By collaborating closely with your development team, you can ensure that your wireframes and prototypes are not only user-friendly but also technically sound.

Communicating Your Vision to Stakeholders

Wireframing and prototyping also play a crucial role in communicating your vision to stakeholders. Whether you are presenting your product to potential investors, partners, or customers, having a tangible prototype can help bring your vision to life and demonstrate the value of your product. A well-designed prototype can make a strong impression and help you secure the support and resources you need to bring your product to market.

Conclusion

Wireframing and prototyping are essential steps in turning your idea into a tangible product. They help you visualize the user experience, test and refine your concepts, and communicate your vision clearly to developers and stakeholders. My experience with EZOS taught me the importance of these processes and how they can transform a simple idea into a multimillion-dollar company. Remember, the key is to start with a clear vision and use the tools and techniques available to bring that vision to life.

One of the most important aspects of wireframing and prototyping is the ability to iterate and improve your designs based on user feedback. This feedback loop is crucial for creating a product that meets the needs of your users and delivers a great user experience. By continuously testing and refining your wireframes and prototypes, you can identify and address issues early in the development process, saving time and resources in the long run.

As you embark on your own entrepreneurial journey, remember to start with a clear vision, use the tools and techniques available, and iterate based on feedback to bring your vision to life. The journey from an initial idea to a fully functional product involves multiple stages of development, and wireframing and prototyping are critical components of this journey. Wireframing helps you lay the groundwork by visualizing the user interface and flow, while prototyping allows you to test and refine these concepts in a more interactive format. By investing time and effort into these processes, you can create a product that meets the needs of your users and stands out in the market.

CHAPTER 7

Defining Your MVP

Being the Most Valuable Player (MVP) was the most important thing I was trying to accomplish when I played college football and in the NFL. Being the MVP in sports means that you were the difference maker, the reason your team won. In technology, the MVP is just as important in your business success trajectory; however, MVP stands for Minimum Viable Product in the tech industry. It signifies the least amount of features your product needs to offer in order to start making money and gaining customers. This concept is fundamental to the initial stages of your tech company and must be well-defined and researched. You need to feel confident in your ability to sell the MVP because it represents your initial investment in the business. Once the money is in and the product is built, it's your job to sell it.

Especially if you aren't a technical founder, the MVP needs to be clearly defined, drawn out, and written with clear communication so the tech team can build exactly what you need. The more you sway and change the MVP requirements, the more the initial investment will cost. However, if you are completely buttoned up and sure about what you need to build to get your first customer, that's your MVP—get it done. Your Minimum Viable Product will end up being your Most Valuable Player as you start this business and will set the stage for the rest of your company as you sell, market, raise capital, and build.

Identifying Core Features

Identifying the core features of your product that will attract initial customers is the first step in defining your MVP. These features should solve the primary pain points of your target market and provide enough value to convince customers to pay for your product. When I was developing EZOS, I focused on solving the issues of real-time updates and efficient invoicing for property managers and vendors. These were the core problems that needed to be addressed immediately to make the product viable in the market.

To determine the MVP essentials, start by listing all the potential features you envision for your product. Then, prioritize these features based on their importance and the value they bring to the customer. The goal is to identify the minimum set of features that can deliver a complete user experience and solve the primary problems identified. I like to rank each feature by probability to affect our immediate revenue. For EZOS, the essential features were real-time progress tracking, automated invoicing and daily summary reports. These features provided immediate value to property managers and vendors, addressing their critical needs and making the product indispensable because of the headaches it solved during student housing turn.

Testing MVP Concepts

Testing MVP concepts is crucial to ensure that your MVP meets the needs of your target market. Create prototypes or mock-ups of your MVP and test them with potential users. Gather feedback to understand what works and what doesn't. This process will help you refine your MVP and make necessary adjustments before the final build. For EZOS, I created a "fake app" with Invision to simulate the functionality and gather feedback from potential users. This approach allowed me to refine the product based on real user input and ensured that the final MVP was well-received. This also allows for us to generate interest and a buzz before the product is ready.

The MVP is not just a minimal version of your product; it's a strategic approach to building a product that can be launched quickly and improved over time based on user feedback. It's your initial stepping stone that will help you gain early adopters, generate revenue, and validate your business idea. Your MVP will be your Most Valuable Player as you start this business and will tell the story of the rest of your company as you sell, market, raise capital, and build.

Understanding Your Target Market

To define your MVP effectively, it's essential to start with a comprehensive understanding of your target market and their needs. Conduct market research to identify the key pain points and challenges your potential customers face. This research will provide valuable insights into the features and functionalities that are most important to your target audience.

Once you have a clear understanding of your target market, create detailed user personas to represent your ideal customers. These personas should include demographic information, job roles, goals, challenges, and how your product can address their needs. By developing detailed personas, you can better understand the specific requirements of your target market and tailor your MVP to meet those needs.

Prioritizing Features

After defining your user personas, it's time to prioritize the features for your MVP. Start by listing all the potential features and functionalities you envision for your product. Then, categorize these features based on their importance, the value they provide to the customer, and likelihood to affect that near future revenue. Focus on the features that address the most critical pain points and deliver the highest value. These will form the core of your MVP.

As you prioritize the features for your MVP, consider the resources and time required to develop each feature. It's essential to strike a balance between delivering a product that meets the needs of your target market and keeping development time and costs manageable. The goal is to create a product that provides enough value to attract early customers while allowing for future iterations and improvements.

Creating Wireframes and Prototypes

Once you have a prioritized list of features, start creating wireframes and prototypes to visualize your MVP. Wireframes provide a basic visual representation of your product's layout and structure, while prototypes offer a more interactive and detailed version of the product. Use tools such as Figma, Sketch, or Adobe XD to create your wireframes and prototypes. These tools allow you to design and iterate on your MVP efficiently.

With your wireframes and prototypes in hand, test your MVP concepts with potential users. Conduct usability testing sessions to gather feedback on the user experience and identify any issues or areas for improvement. Pay close attention to how users interact with the product and the feedback they provide. Use this feedback to refine your MVP and make necessary adjustments.

Collaborating With Your Development Team

Throughout the testing process, it's crucial to maintain open communication with your development team. Ensure that they understand the goals and priorities of the MVP and are aligned with the vision for the product. Regularly review progress and address any technical challenges or roadblocks that may arise. Collaboration and clear communication with your development team are key to successfully building and launching your MVP.

Launching Your MVP

Once your MVP is built, it's time to launch it to your target market. Develop a go-to-market strategy that includes marketing, sales, and customer support plans. Focus on reaching your target audience through channels where they are most active, whether it's social media, industry forums, or email marketing. Highlight the key features and benefits of your MVP and how it addresses the pain points of your target market.

Monitor the performance of your MVP closely after launch. Track key metrics such as user engagement, retention rates, and customer feedback. Use this data to identify areas for improvement and prioritize future updates and enhancements. Remember, the MVP is just the beginning. Continuously iterate and improve your product based on user feedback and market demands.

Continuous Improvement and Adaptation

In summary, defining your MVP involves a strategic approach to building a product that addresses the most critical needs of your target market. Start by understanding your target audience and their pain points, then prioritize the features that deliver the highest value. Create wireframes and prototypes to visualize your MVP, test it with potential users, and gather feedback for refinement. Maintain open communication with your development team and develop a go-to-market strategy for a successful launch. Continuously monitor performance and iterate on your product to ensure long-term success.

Defining and building your MVP is a crucial step in the journey of creating a successful tech company. It sets the foundation for future growth and allows you to validate your business idea with real customers. By focusing on delivering a product that meets the needs of your target market and provides real value, you can attract early adopters, generate revenue, and build a strong foundation for your business.

As you embark on this journey, remember that the MVP is just the beginning. It's a starting point that allows you to learn, iterate, and improve your product based on user feedback and market demands. Stay focused on your vision, be open to feedback, and continuously strive to deliver the best possible product to your customers. With a well-defined MVP, you are well on your way to building a successful and sustainable tech company.

In my own experience with EZOS, defining the MVP was a critical step that set the stage for our success. By focusing on solving the core problems of real-time updates and efficient invoicing, we were able to create a product that provided immediate value to our target market and allowed for us to have paying customers, Day 1. This initial success allowed us to attract early customers, generate revenue, and validate our business idea. From there, we continued to iterate and improve our product based on user feedback, leading to the growth and success of EZOS.

As you define your MVP, keep in mind the importance of staying agile and adaptable. The tech industry is constantly evolving, and customer needs can change over time. By maintaining a focus on delivering value and being open to feedback, you can ensure that your product remains relevant and competitive in the market.

In conclusion, defining your MVP is a strategic process that involves understanding your target market, prioritizing features, and continuously iterating based on feedback. It's a critical step in building a successful tech company and sets the foundation for future growth and success. By staying focused on delivering value and being open to feedback, you can create a product that meets the needs of your customers and drives the success of your business.

CHAPTER 8

Building Your Development Team

When I had a clear understanding of my MVP, the next crucial step was finding someone who could bring my vision to life. As a nontechnical founder, I had the vision, but executing the product required trust in others. There are several ways to approach this. You can hire a local dev shop, which will be more expensive but probably more comfortable for a first-time nontechnical founder. Alternatively, you can hire an overseas technical dev shop, which will be cheaper but likely come with some frustrations. Another option is to hire your own developer(s) internally and put them on salary. This approach is best suited for a second-time tech founder in my opinion or if you have mentorship from someone who has managed devs before as a first-time tech founder.

When creating my first tech company, I had no idea what I was doing but had a clear vision of what I wanted to create and who I was going to sell it to. I opted to go with a local dev shop for my initial tech company. I decided on this route because I wanted to sit down and meet with them regularly, discuss vision and progress, and hold them accountable to deadlines and product deliveries. The closer they were to me, the more control I felt I had over the process and understood where my investment was going.

I went to each dev shop in the local area and shopped the offers around to get the best price for my proposal, essentially creating a small bidding war between the local dev shops for this project and my money. This turned out to be a great decision because it was easy to communicate with them, we had regular meetings, and I learned how to manage a technical product, talk in technical terms, and understand the jargon required when creating an app or software. Additionally, I appreciated this decision because I got the best price and they were flexible with how I could pay. I recommend setting up payment terms around product deliveries to ensure accountability and steady progress.

Finding and hiring the right developers or a dev shop to bring your MVP to life is a critical step. First, sourcing developers involves understanding where to look and what to look for. Local dev shops can be found through networking, industry events, and online searches. Hiring overseas developers can be done through platforms such as Upwork or Freelancer, but it's essential to vet them thoroughly. Internal hires can be sourced from job boards, tech meetups, or through referrals.

Writing an effective request for proposal (RFP) is the next step. An RFP should clearly outline your project's goals, scope, timeline, and include your wireframes at minimum. Leave out budget because you want them to tell you what cost they will do the work for. It should also include specific questions for the dev shops or developers to answer, which will help you assess their suitability for your project. The more detailed and clear your RFP, the better responses you will receive, making it easier to choose the right partner for your MVP.

Budgeting and timelines are also crucial elements. Understanding how much you are willing to spend is the most important piece of shopping, your RFP. When budgeting, consider not just the development costs but also potential revisions, updates, and ongoing maintenance. Timelines should account for development, testing, and any unforeseen delays. Setting milestones and payment schedules tied to these milestones ensures that you only pay for work completed and that there is a clear path to project completion. I recommend not paying by the hours but instead keeping it as a flat rate for specific milestones.

In my experience, choosing a local dev shop provided numerous benefits. It facilitated easy communication, allowed for regular in-person meetings, and helped me learn how to manage a technical product. This approach also offered flexibility in payment terms, which was beneficial as I navigated the financial aspects of my start-up. Creating a small bidding war between local dev shops also ensured that I received the best possible price for my project.

Building your development team is a foundational step in bringing your MVP to life. Whether you choose a local dev shop, an overseas team, or internal hires, the key is to clearly define your vision, communicate effectively, and manage the process diligently. My journey with EZOS taught me the importance of these elements and how they contribute to transforming a vision into a tangible, successful product.

The process of building your development team should begin with a thorough understanding of what you need in terms of skills and expertise. If your project requires a particular technology stack, ensure that your developers have experience with that stack. Look for portfolios and case studies that demonstrate their capability in handling projects similar to yours. This will give you confidence in their ability to deliver your vision.

With Gard, I opted to hire because I had the skillset to manage devs by the time I started that project. For those opting to hire internally, finding the right talent can be challenging but rewarding. Internal hires become an integral part of your company culture and can grow with your business. To attract top talent, you need to not only offer competitive salaries and benefits but also sell them on your vision and the impact of the project. Most of the times founders can't provide competitive salaries, so incentivizing with stock in the company is a best practice to supplement what you can pay. Engaging with local tech communities, attending hackathons, and leveraging your professional network can help you find candidates who are passionate about what you're building.

When hiring overseas, it is crucial to establish clear communication channels and expectations. Time zone differences can pose a challenge, so it's essential to set up regular check-ins and use project management tools such as Jira, Trello, or Asana to keep everyone on the same page. Overcommunicating can help mitigate misunderstandings and ensure that the project stays on track. Using collaboration tools such as Slack or Microsoft Teams can also foster better communication and teamwork.

Creating a robust onboarding process for your development team is another critical step. Make sure they understand the company's mission, values, and the specific goals of the project. Provide them with all the necessary resources, including documentation, access to systems, and any tools they need to do their job effectively. A well-structured onboarding process sets the tone for their work and helps them integrate smoothly into your tech company.

As your project progresses, maintain a focus on quality assurance and testing. Regularly test the product to identify and fix bugs early. This not only improves the product's quality but also saves time and resources in the long run. Implementing a continuous integration and continuous deployment (CI/CD) pipeline can streamline this process, allowing for automated testing and faster iterations.

Feedback loops are essential for the successful development of your MVP. Encourage your team to provide feedback on the development process and any challenges they encounter. This open line of communication helps address issues promptly and fosters a collaborative environment where everyone feels invested in the project's success. Additionally, gathering feedback from users during the testing phases provides invaluable insights that can guide further development.

As the CEO or project lead, your role is to ensure that the project stays on course. This involves regular progress reviews, adjusting timelines as needed, and managing the budget effectively. Being hands-on and approachable can significantly impact your team's morale and productivity. Celebrate milestones and recognize the hard work of your team to keep them motivated.

Building a development team also means preparing for scalability. As your product grows, so will the demands on your team. Plan for future growth by creating a scalable architecture and considering how additional features will be integrated into the product. This foresight helps prevent technical debt and ensures that your product can evolve with market demands. With EZOS I didn't know anything about scalable architecture, but essentially it means at the busiest moment of use can your system not break. So, as CEO you need to clearly tell your dev team what an example would be of heavy usage so they can build with that expectation in mind.

In my own journey with EZOS, the process of building a development team was a learning experience that shaped the success of the company. Starting with a local dev shop provided the hands-on interaction and learning opportunity I needed as a nontechnical founder. Over time, as the product evolved, we transitioned to a more hybrid model, incorporating internal hires and leveraging overseas talent for specific tasks. This approach allowed us to balance cost, quality, and scalability effectively.

In conclusion, building your development team is a critical step that requires careful planning, clear communication, and strategic decision-making. Whether you choose a local dev shop, overseas developers, or internal hires, the key is to align everyone with your vision, manage the process diligently, and maintain a focus on quality and scalability. By taking these steps, you can bring your MVP to life and set the foundation for a successful tech company long into the future.

Embarking on the journey of building your development team can be daunting, but it is also one of the most rewarding aspects of launching a tech start-up. The right team not only brings your vision to life but also becomes a vital part of your company's culture and success. Remember, the goal is not just to build a product but also to create a sustainable business that can grow and adapt to the ever-changing tech landscape. By focusing on collaboration, continuous improvement, and maintaining a clear vision, you can navigate the challenges and build a development team that drives your company toward success.

CHAPTER 9

Setting Up Development Tools

Providing developers with the tools they need is crucial to the success of your tech project. This process typically involves the developers informing you of their requirements, and your responsibility is to ensure they have everything they need. While I may not have the most extensive technical knowledge, I can share the tools our team uses to manage our projects efficiently. We rely on Amazon Web Services (AWS) for hosting, JIRA for ticket management, Expo for app development, Apple Developer Account, Google Play Developer Account, and Slack for team communication. These tools help streamline our operations and maintain a smooth workflow.

It's important to note that there are various tech stacks available that can replace these apps and software. The key takeaway for any first-time tech founder is to ensure that you have ownership and admin privileges on all these platforms. This allows you to maintain some control over a process that might be foreign to you but is essential for your company. Maintaining ownership means that if your dev team quits or you need to fire them, you can have someone else pick up where they left off. You don't want to have to restart work that has already been completed.

Setting up developer accounts is the first step. For mobile apps, you need to have Apple Developer and Google Play Developer accounts. These accounts allow you to publish your app on the respective app stores and are essential for distributing your app to users. These platforms also provide tools and resources for app development, testing, and analytics. Creating these accounts requires an annual fee, but they are necessary investments for getting your app to market.

Next, you need a reliable hosting platform. We use AWS for hosting. AWS is widely used because it is scalable, reliable, and offers a range of services that can support your app's backend infrastructure. Whether you need storage, databases, or computing power, AWS provides solutions that can grow with your app. Setting up an AWS account and understanding its basic services can seem daunting, but it's a crucial step in ensuring that your app runs smoothly. AWS also offers extensive documentation and support to help you get started.

Project management tools are also essential for keeping your development process organized and on track. We use JIRA for ticket management. JIRA allows us to create tasks, assign them to team members, set deadlines, and track progress. It helps in managing the workflow and ensures that everyone is on the same page. Effective use of project management tools can significantly improve your team's productivity and keep the development process transparent. JIRA also integrates with other tools like Slack, which enhances our overall efficiency.

For team communication, we rely on Slack. Slack is an excellent tool for real-time communication and collaboration. It allows team members to communicate quickly, share files, and integrate with other tools we use, such as JIRA and AWS. Keeping communication channels open and organized is vital for a smooth development process. Slack channels can be created for different projects or teams, making it easier to manage conversations and information flow.

Another critical aspect of setting up development tools is ensuring that there is a place where the code is pushed regularly. For external dev shops, it's important to have a system where they push the code they write every week or two. This ensures that you own the code and know where to access it. Platforms such as GitHub or Google Drive can be used to store the source code securely. This practice not only helps in maintaining the continuity of the project but also allows you to monitor the progress and ensure that the development is on track.

Using GitHub for version control is a best practice in software development. It allows multiple developers to work on the code simultaneously, track changes, and collaborate more effectively. Regularly pushing code to a repository ensures that all changes are documented and that you have a backup of your codebase. GitHub also provides features such as pull requests and code reviews, which are valuable for maintaining code quality and facilitating collaboration.

It's crucial to have control over these tools and accounts to safeguard your project. In my experience, having admin privileges and ownership of all development tools and platforms has been invaluable. It provides a safety net in case there are changes in your development team, and it ensures that the project can continue without significant disruptions. This level of control also allows you to make informed decisions about the project's direction and manage access to sensitive information.

Security is another important consideration when setting up development tools. Ensure that all accounts have strong, unique passwords and enable two-factor authentication (2FA) where possible. This adds an extra layer of security and protects your project from unauthorized access. Regularly review account permissions and remove access for team members who no longer need it. Keeping your tools and platforms secure is essential for protecting your intellectual property (IP) and maintaining the integrity of your project.

In conclusion, setting up the necessary tools and accounts for your development team is a foundational step in the development process. By securing developer accounts, choosing reliable hosting platforms, using effective project management tools, and maintaining ownership and control over all these resources, you can ensure that your project runs smoothly and efficiently. These tools not only facilitate the development process but also provide the necessary infrastructure to support your app's growth and success. My journey with EZOS highlighted the importance of these steps, and they have been instrumental in transforming a vision into a tangible, successful product.

Providing developers with the right tools is not just about fulfilling their technical requirements; it's about empowering them to do their best work. When developers have access to the right resources, they can focus on building and refining your product rather than dealing with technical roadblocks. This results in a more efficient development process and a higher quality end product.

One aspect that is often overlooked is the importance of documentation. Ensure that all tools, processes, and workflows are well-documented. This includes setting up and configuring accounts, using project management tools, and guidelines for code management. Good documentation serves as a reference for current team members and helps onboard new members more quickly. It also ensures consistency in how tools are used and processes are followed.

As your project progresses, regularly review the tools and processes you have in place. Technology is constantly evolving, and new tools may offer better solutions or improved efficiencies. Be open to adopting new technologies that can enhance your development process. Encourage your team to provide feedback on the tools they use and suggest improvements. This continuous improvement mindset ensures that you are always leveraging the best resources available.

In my experience, setting up and managing development tools is an ongoing process. As your project grows and evolves, so will your needs. Being proactive in managing these tools and staying informed about new developments in technology will help you maintain a competitive edge. Remember, the goal is to create an environment where your developers can thrive and deliver their best work.

Finally, don't underestimate the importance of a positive and collaborative team culture. While tools and processes are essential, the people using them are your most valuable asset. Foster a culture of open communication, mutual respect, and continuous learning. Encourage your team to share their knowledge and support each other. This collaborative environment will not only enhance productivity but also contribute to a more fulfilling and enjoyable work experience for everyone involved.

In summary, setting up development tools involves more than just providing technical resources. It requires careful planning, continuous management, and a focus on security and documentation. By creating a supportive and well-equipped environment for your developers, you set the stage for a successful and efficient development process. My journey with EZOS taught me the importance of these elements, and they have been instrumental in transforming a vision into a successful product. As you embark on your own journey, remember that the right tools and a strong team culture are key to achieving your goals.

PART 3

Building Your Brand and Market Presence

CHAPTER 10

Reserving Online Spaces and Branding

The name and brand of your company are crucial decisions in the creation of a tech company. My suggestion is to pick the name first and then see if it is available on social media handles, websites, and other online platforms. Picking a tech name should come naturally to you. Spend time jotting down different name ideas over the course of weeks or months, and eventually, one will stand out to you as the one you should use. When creating a brand new product and a brand new idea, I personally think it's important to have a name that gives people an idea of what you offer or solve. This approach can be particularly helpful when selling your product, as it's already challenging to get someone to respond to an email. If the name of your company can do a little talking for you, it can smoothen out people's reception to learning more.

Not all companies follow this naming convention, but I suggest that if you ever need to change the name, remember that names aren't permanent. The ability to evolve your brand and product over time will become a conversation as you scale. For instance, we started off as EZTurn because we wanted to create an app that made student housing turnover easier than ever before. We chose that name because people in that industry would understand our mission right away when they heard our name. However, as we grew, we realized that the name EZTurn was limiting our sales capabilities outside of student housing and even within it for upselling additional services. We have since changed the name to EZOS because we provide so much more value outside of just turnover processes.

Reserving your online handles and domains is an essential step once you have your name. Claim your online handles as close to your company name as possible. While I don't think the social handle is as important as the business or product name itself, it still plays a significant role in your overall branding strategy. Make sure to secure your domain name early on. This ensures that you have a professional web presence that matches your brand. A good domain name should be easy to remember, easy to spell, and as close to your company name as possible.

Social media strategy is another critical component of your branding efforts. Social media platforms are powerful tools for reaching your audience, building brand awareness, and engaging with potential customers. Once you have your company name, check its availability across major social media platforms such as Twitter, Facebook, Instagram, and LinkedIn. Consistent social media handles help reinforce your brand identity and make it easier for people to find and follow you. Even if you don't plan to use all these platforms immediately, securing the handles ensures that you have them available for future use.

Logo design is another vital element of your branding. Your logo is often the first visual representation of your brand that people see, so it needs to be compelling and reflective of your company's identity and values. When designing your logo, think about how it will look across different mediums, from your website and social media profiles to business cards and marketing materials. A good logo should be simple, memorable, and versatile. You may want to work with a professional designer to ensure that your logo effectively communicates your brand's essence.

When we started EZOS, we made sure to secure our domain and social media handles early on. This helped establish our online presence and made it easier for customers to find us. As we transitioned to EZOS, we repeated this process to ensure that our new brand was just as well-represented online. Our logo evolved too, reflecting our broader mission of making operations easier across various industries, not just student housing.

In addition to reserving your domain and social media handles, it's important to build a consistent brand image across all platforms. This includes using the same colors, fonts, and design elements in your website, social media profiles, and marketing materials. Consistency helps create a strong brand identity and makes your company more recognizable. A well-designed brand book can guide your team in maintaining this consistency as your company grows.

Another aspect of branding is your company's voice and messaging. Define the tone and style of your communication. Is it formal or casual? Professional or playful? Your brand's voice should reflect your company's values and resonate with your target audience. This consistency in messaging will help build trust and loyalty among your customers.

In today's digital age, having a robust online presence is critical. Your website is often the first point of contact for potential customers. Make sure it is user-friendly, informative, and visually appealing. Invest in good website design and ensure that your content is engaging and provides value to your visitors. Regularly update your website with new content, such as blog posts, case studies, and testimonials, to keep it fresh and relevant.

Search engine optimization (SEO) is another important aspect of building your online presence. SEO helps improve your website's visibility in search engine results, making it easier for potential customers to find you. Use relevant keywords in your website content, meta descriptions, and blog posts. High-quality content that answers your audience's questions can help improve your search rankings and drive more traffic to your site.

Email marketing is another powerful tool for building your brand and engaging with your audience. Collect email addresses through your website and social media channels and send regular newsletters to keep your audience informed about your latest updates, offers, and content. Personalized and targeted email campaigns can help nurture leads and convert them into loyal customers.

Public relations (PR) can also play a significant role in building your brand. Media coverage in industry publications, blogs, and news outlets can increase your visibility and credibility. Develop relationships with journalists and influencers in your industry and pitch them interesting stories about your company, product, or industry insights.

Networking is another important aspect of building your brand. Attend industry events, conferences, and meetups to connect with potential customers, partners, and influencers. Networking can help you gain valuable insights, build relationships, and create opportunities for collaboration and growth.

As your company grows, your branding efforts should evolve as well. Regularly review your branding strategy and make adjustments as needed to stay relevant and resonate with your target audience. Your brand should reflect your company's growth and evolution, and staying flexible and adaptable is key to maintaining a strong brand presence.

In conclusion, reserving your domain and social media handles and developing a compelling brand for your tech company are critical steps in establishing your business. Your company name should convey your mission or the problem you solve, making it easier to attract interest and communicate your value proposition. While names can evolve, the importance of securing your online presence and creating a strong brand identity remains constant. By focusing on these elements, you lay a solid foundation for your company's growth and success. My experience with EZOS has shown me that thoughtful branding and securing your online spaces can significantly impact your company's ability to connect with customers and scale effectively.

Creating a strong brand involves more than just a catchy name and a good logo. It requires a strategic approach to building your online presence, engaging with your audience, and maintaining consistency across all platforms. By investing time and effort into your branding efforts, you can create a lasting impression and build a loyal customer base. As you embark on your journey to build your tech company, remember that a strong brand is one of your most valuable assets. It sets you apart from the competition, builds trust with your customers, and paves the way for long-term success.

CHAPTER 11

Building a Sales Target List

Building a comprehensive sales target list is a critical step in ensuring the success of your tech company. The foundation of this process is having a clearly defined ideal customer profile (ICP). Your ICP should represent the type of customer that is the easiest to sell to initially—those who experience the specific problems your software aims to solve. This profile includes detailed information such as their position, age, the company they work for, the problems they face, and how your software can alleviate those issues. Once you have a detailed understanding of your ICP, you can begin identifying potential customers who fit this profile and adding them to your target list.

In my experience, using simple tools such as Google Sheets or Excel to build your initial target list is both cost-effective and efficient. While more sophisticated tools such as Salesforce or other CRM (Customer Relationship Management) systems can be beneficial, they often come with a higher cost. For a start-up, it's wise to minimize expenses until you start generating revenue. Begin by spending time each week researching and adding new prospects to your list. This involves looking at LinkedIn profiles, company websites, and industry forums to gather relevant information about potential customers.

Attending conferences and industry events where your ICP congregates is another effective way to build your target list. These events provide opportunities to meet potential customers face-to-face, gain insights into their challenges, and understand their needs on a deeper level. While online research is valuable, these in-person interactions can offer a richer understanding of your target audience.

When we started with EZOS, we initially believed that property managers would be our primary customers, as they dealt directly with the problems our software solved. However, through our sales efforts, we quickly learned that property managers often lacked the authority to make purchasing decisions. This insight forced us to shift our focus to higher-level executives, such as COOs (Chief Operating Officers), who had the power to implement solutions across multiple properties. This adjustment in our ICP was crucial for our sales strategy.

Creating a sales funnel is an essential next step after identifying your sales targets. A sales funnel helps you visualize and manage the journey from potential lead to paying customer. The funnel starts broad at the top, including all your potential leads, and narrows down as leads move through stages of qualification, engagement, and conversion. Initially, you will have a large number of leads at the top of the funnel. As you engage with these leads and learn more about their needs and purchasing capabilities, you can narrow down the list to focus on the most promising prospects.

A CRM strategy is vital for managing your interactions with potential customers. While a simple Google Sheet or Excel file can be sufficient for tracking interactions and follow-ups in the early stages, transitioning to a more robust CRM system as your customer base grows can help you manage your sales pipeline more efficiently. CRMs allow you to keep detailed records of your communications, schedule follow-ups, and analyze sales data, which can help improve your sales strategy over time.

In my journey with EZOS, I dedicated significant time to prospecting and understanding potential customers. This involved not just identifying the right contacts but also researching their specific challenges and needs. LinkedIn was a valuable resource for finding key decision makers and gaining insights into their professional backgrounds and current roles. Company websites and industry reports also provided valuable information about potential customers' pain points and business priorities.

Building a sales target list is not a one-time task but an ongoing process. Continuously adding new prospects, refining your ICP based on feedback and market changes, and nurturing relationships with potential customers are all essential steps. Your sales strategy should be flexible and evolve as you gain more insights into your market and customer needs.

One important aspect of this process is email marketing. Once you have your target list, start reaching out to these individuals through personalized email campaigns. Your emails should highlight how your software can solve their specific problems and include a clear call to action, such as setting up a meeting or demo. Personalization is key to making your emails stand out and increasing the likelihood of a response.

Prospecting lists can also be sourced from industry conferences and events. These gatherings are not only opportunities to network but also to gather attendee lists, which can be valuable for future outreach. If attending events in person is not feasible, consider participating in virtual conferences and webinars, which can also provide access to attendee information.

It's also crucial to continually engage with your existing prospects and customers. Regular follow-ups, updates about new features or improvements to your software, and personalized communication can help build strong relationships and increase the likelihood of conversion. Use feedback from these interactions to refine your sales pitch and improve your product.

As you grow your sales target list, it's important to maintain detailed records of your interactions. This includes noting any feedback, questions, or concerns raised by potential customers. These insights can help you better understand their needs and tailor your sales approach accordingly. Keeping track of follow-up dates and ensuring timely communication shows professionalism and can make a significant difference in building trust with your prospects.

In conclusion, building a sales target list involves a deep understanding of your ICP, thorough research, and consistent engagement with potential customers. By starting with simple tools, attending industry events, and leveraging email marketing, you can create a robust list of prospects. Continuously refine your approach based on feedback and market changes to ensure that your sales strategy remains effective. My experience with EZOS taught me that understanding your customers deeply and being adaptable in your sales approach are key to building a strong and effective sales pipeline.

CHAPTER 12

Marketing and Sales Strategies for Tech Start-Ups

Marketing and sales are the lifeblood of any tech start-up. You can have the best product in the world, but without a strategy to attract customers and close deals, your product will go unnoticed. In this chapter, we will explore the fundamental marketing and sales strategies that tech start-ups need to master to build awareness, create demand, and develop a scalable sales pipeline.

Building a Brand Identity That Stands Out

Before diving into tactical marketing, you need to ensure that your brand has a strong identity. A brand isn't just a logo or a color scheme —it's the emotional connection customers have with your product. For tech start-ups, brand identity plays a crucial role in establishing trust and differentiation, especially in competitive markets where potential customers need to know why your solution stands out.

When building your brand, focus on your mission and values. Think about what you want to represent to your customers. Are you innovative, customer-centric, or industry-disruptive? Make sure these values shine through in every interaction, whether it's on your website, social media, or in the way your sales team communicates.

Having a clear and consistent brand identity helps your audience connect with you on a deeper level. It's not just about selling a product; it's about offering a solution they can trust. The stronger your brand identity, the easier it will be to attract your target audience and keep them engaged.

Understanding Your Customers: Profiles and Segmentation

Every marketing strategy starts with understanding your audience. For tech start-ups, it's essential to develop detailed customer profiles—often referred to as personas. These profiles should describe your ideal customers' demographics, behaviors, challenges, and goals. By fully understanding who your customers are, you'll be able to create messaging that resonates deeply with them.

Once you have defined your personas, you can take it a step further by segmenting your audience. Segmentation allows you to divide your audience into smaller groups based on shared characteristics such as industry, company size, or even purchasing behavior. This targeted approach enables you to create personalized marketing messages that address the specific needs of each group.

For example, if your tech solution serves both small business owners and large enterprises, the way you market to them should differ. Small business owners might be more concerned with cost savings and ease of use, while enterprises might care more about scalability and advanced features. By tailoring your messaging to the distinct needs of each segment, you increase your chances of connecting with them and moving them down your sales funnel.

Digital Marketing Channels for Start-Ups

Once you've built a strong brand and identified your target audience, it's time to leverage digital marketing channels to spread the word. Digital marketing is vital for tech start-ups because it allows you to reach a broad audience at a relatively low cost compared to traditional advertising. Here are a few key channels you should focus on:

- **SEO**: Organic traffic from search engines is one of the most effective ways to attract visitors to your website. By optimizing your content for relevant keywords, you can ensure that your website shows up when potential customers are searching for solutions to their problems. For example, if your start-up provides cybersecurity software for small businesses, you want your website to rank high when someone searches "best cybersecurity software for small businesses."

- **Pay-Per-Click (PPC) Advertising**: PPC allows you to get in front of your target audience quickly. With platforms such as Google Ads, you can bid on relevant keywords to ensure that your ads appear at the top of search results. This is especially helpful for start-ups that need immediate visibility, such as during a product launch.

- **Social Media Marketing**: Platforms such as LinkedIn, Twitter, and Facebook offer excellent opportunities for tech start-ups to engage with potential customers. LinkedIn is especially valuable for B2B (Businesses who sale to other businesses) start-ups, where you can directly target decision makers in the industries you serve. Social media also allows for interaction and customer engagement, making it a great tool for building relationships and trust.

- **Content Marketing**: Providing valuable content such as blog posts, whitepapers, webinars, and case studies helps position your company as a thought leader. When you offer useful information, prospects are more likely to trust you and consider your product when making purchasing decisions. This also improves your SEO, driving more organic traffic to your site.

Using a combination of these channels creates a robust digital presence, allowing you to engage potential customers wherever they are online.

Creating a Strong Sales Funnel

Building awareness is just the first step. Once you've attracted potential customers, you need to guide them through the sales funnel, turning interest into action. The stages of the sales funnel include awareness, consideration, and decision.

- **Awareness**: At this stage, potential customers are just becoming aware of your product. They may not know much about it, so your goal is to spark interest. This can be achieved through content marketing, social media posts, or paid advertising. The key here is to educate them on the problem your product solves, which creates the initial connection.
- **Consideration**: In this phase, your prospects are now actively considering your product as a solution. To move them further down the funnel, you can offer free trials, demos, or webinars that demonstrate how your product works. Email marketing also plays a crucial role at this stage, where you nurture leads by sending them relevant information tailored to their needs.
- **Decision**: The final stage is where prospects are ready to make a purchase. Here, it's important to ensure that the buying process is simple and clear. Your sales team should focus on providing personalized offers or discounts to close the deal, and your website should have an easy-to-navigate checkout process for those who prefer self-service.

By creating a clear and structured sales funnel, you can systematically move prospects toward becoming paying customers.

Measuring Success and Optimizing Campaigns

One of the greatest advantages of digital marketing is the ability to measure results in real time. Tracking key performance indicators (KPIs) such as click-through rates, conversion rates, and customer acquisition costs allows you to see what's working and what isn't. Using this data, you can make informed decisions about where to allocate resources, refine messaging, or adjust targeting.

For instance, if you notice that a particular campaign is bringing in leads but they aren't converting into sales, you might need to tweak your messaging or adjust your offer. Conversely, if a campaign is performing well, you can increase your budget for that campaign to maximize results.

Ongoing testing and optimization are crucial to scaling your marketing efforts effectively. Tools such as Google Analytics, Hub-Spot, or even custom CRM dashboards allow you to track campaign performance and optimize accordingly.

Avoiding Common Mistakes

While implementing your marketing and sales strategies, it's easy to fall into a few common traps. One mistake that many start-ups make is targeting too broad an audience. While it may seem like casting a wide net will bring in more leads, it's usually more effective to focus on a specific niche where you can stand out as a market leader.

Another common pitfall is relying too heavily on initial outreach without enough follow up. Marketing isn't a "one and done" activity—successful campaigns often require multiple touchpoints. Make sure you have a process in place for nurturing leads, whether through follow-up emails, retargeting ads, or personal outreach from your sales team.

Preparing for Cold Outreach and More Targeted Approaches

At this point, we've covered the broader marketing strategies that build awareness and bring potential customers into your funnel. But what about reaching out to prospects who aren't yet aware of your brand or product? That's where cold outreach comes into play, and it's one of the most effective ways to reach new markets directly.

In the next chapter, we will dive deeper into cold outreach and how to craft personalized messaging that resonates with your target audience. You'll learn how to develop a cold outreach strategy that complements the broader marketing efforts we've covered here, driving both immediate and long-term sales growth.

CHAPTER 13

Cold Outreach and Marketing Techniques

When you're building a tech start-up, one of the most challenging aspects is getting your product in front of the right people. Whether you're trying to land your first customers, attract investors, or build strategic partnerships, cold outreach can be an incredibly effective tool. However, there's a science to doing it well. In this chapter, we'll break down how to structure and execute a successful cold outreach strategy—one that not only gets you noticed but gets you results.

Cold outreach, by its very nature, involves reaching out to people who may have never heard of your company or product. While this may sound intimidating, it's a critical part of scaling your start-up, especially when your product is still gaining traction. If done correctly, cold outreach can open doors that would otherwise remain shut.

Crafting the Perfect Cold Email

When it comes to cold outreach, email is still one of the most powerful tools at your disposal. But with crowded inboxes and short attention spans, the way you craft your email is critical. Here's how you can create a cold email that captures attention and compels the recipient to take action.

1. **The Subject Line**: This is your first—and possibly only—chance to grab the recipient's attention. A subject line should be brief but compelling. Avoid generic lines like "Introducing [Company Name]" or "Can we connect?" Instead, use a subject line that is either personalized or focused on value. For example: "Quick idea to improve your [specific goal]" or "How [their competitor] is saving 20 percent with tech."

2. **The Opening Sentence**: After the subject line, the first sentence of your email is the second most important element. This is where personalization comes into play. Address the recipient by name and make it clear why you're reaching out to them specifically. Reference something relevant to their business, role, or recent activity (e.g., "I noticed your recent product launch...") to demonstrate that your email isn't just a mass template.

3. **The Value Proposition**: The body of your email should be concise and focused on what value you bring to the recipient. Avoid long paragraphs and jargon. Focus on the recipient's pain points and how your product or solution can address them. For example: "Our platform automates [specific task], helping companies like yours save 10 hours a week."

4. **Call to Action (CTA)**: Every cold email should have a clear call to action, whether it's asking for a brief 10-minute meeting or offering to send additional information. The CTA should be easy to say yes to—don't ask for too much upfront. Example: "Could we schedule a quick call next week to see if this might be a fit for your team?"

5. **The Follow-Up**: One of the most overlooked aspects of cold outreach is the follow-up. Research shows that many deals are closed after multiple follow-ups, not after the first email. If you don't get a response initially, send a polite follow-up three to five days later, referencing your original message.

Sequencing Your Emails

Cold outreach is rarely successful after a single attempt. That's where email sequences come into play. A well-structured sequence allows you to build rapport with your target and increase your chances of engagement. Here's a basic example of an effective sequence:

1. **Email 1—Initial Value Pitch**: As described before, this is your introduction email with a value proposition and CTA.

2. **Email 2—Reminder With Added Value** (Day 3 to 5): Reference your original message and add an additional point of value. This could be a case study, a testimonial, or a recent success story from a client in their industry.

3. **Email 3—Gentle Nudge** (Day 7 to 10): Keep it short and polite. Reiterate the value of connecting and suggest a time for a quick call or demo. Example: "I'd love to help you save time with [solution], do you have 10 minutes to chat?"

4. **Email 4—The Break-Up Email** (Day 12 to 15): If they haven't responded by now, send a final message letting them know you won't follow up again, but that you're happy to chat if their priorities change. Example: "I haven't heard back, so I'll assume the timing isn't right. If you're open to it, I'd still love to connect when you're ready."

With a thoughtful sequence, you maximize your chances of getting a response without being overly aggressive. Remember, cold outreach is about persistence, not pressure.

Going Beyond Email: Multichannel Outreach

While cold emails are a powerful tool, limiting your outreach to email alone can reduce your chances of success. A multichannel approach helps ensure that you're engaging potential leads in the way that resonates with them most.

1. **LinkedIn**: If your target audience is in the B2B space, LinkedIn is invaluable. After sending your cold email, try connecting with your target on LinkedIn, referencing the email in a brief message. Don't just copy and paste your email here—LinkedIn messages should be shorter and more casual. Example: "Hi [Name], I sent you an email a few days ago about [briefly describe your solution]. I'd love to connect here and see if we can chat further!"

2. **Direct Messages (DMs)**: Social media platforms such as Twitter or Instagram can also be used for outreach, especially for B2C

(Businesses who sale to consumers) start-ups or those targeting influencers. DMs should be personalized and relevant, and while they may not replace email outreach, they can help you get on the radar of hard-to-reach individuals.

3. **Cold Calling**: While less common in the digital age, cold calling can still be effective in certain industries, particularly when dealing with smaller businesses or niche markets. The key is to keep your call short and focused on providing immediate value. Offer a clear reason for the call and propose a short conversation to discuss their needs.

Using a combination of these channels allows you to cover more ground and increases the likelihood that your message will resonate with your target.

Personalization: The Key to Success

One of the biggest mistakes start-ups make with cold outreach is relying on generic templates. Personalization is critical to standing out in today's crowded market. A one-size-fits-all email is easy to spot—and easy to ignore. To improve your chances of success, tailor each message to the individual recipient.

Look for details that can make your outreach more personal:

- Reference recent achievements, such as funding rounds, product launches, or awards.
- Mention mutual connections or industry events they've attended.
- Personalize based on their role, responsibilities, or specific challenges they might be facing.

For example, if you're reaching out to a CTO (Chief Technology Officer), you might focus on the technical advantages of your solution, whereas a CEO may be more interested in the business outcomes.

Personalization takes more time, but it significantly improves open rates, response rates, and overall success.

What to Do After Outreach

Cold outreach doesn't end when someone responds. What you do after the outreach is just as important. The first response you get from a lead is the beginning of a relationship, not the end.

1. **Manage Responses**: When someone responds positively to your outreach, don't wait too long to follow up. Respond quickly to maintain momentum and schedule a call or meeting as soon as possible. Be sure to address any questions they have and be prepared to dive deeper into the benefits of your product.

2. **Handle Objections**: Not every response will be positive. You might face objections such as "we don't have the budget," or "we're already using a similar solution." This is where you need to have a plan. Don't see objections as rejection—view them as an opportunity to clarify how your product is different or more valuable. Ask follow-up questions like, "What would make you consider switching?" to learn more about their specific needs.

3. **Nurturing Relationships**: Even if the timing isn't right for some prospects, keep them on your radar. Add them to your email list for future updates, share content that might interest them, and periodically check in. Cold outreach can be the first step in building a long-term relationship.

Transitioning Into Your Sales Process

Once your cold outreach efforts start gaining traction, it's time to transition your leads into your formal sales process. This could involve scheduling a product demo, setting up a meeting, or introducing them to your customer success team. Your goal is to continue building trust while moving your prospect closer to making a buying decision.

In **Chapter 14**, we will focus on how to create compelling sales presentations, demos, and investor pitch decks. With the foundation of cold outreach now established, it's time to refine the way you showcase your product and secure those all-important deals.

PART 4

Preparing for Launch and Growth

CHAPTER 14

Creating Sales and Investor Pitch Decks

Creating a compelling sales deck is essential for introducing your product to potential customers. Whether you're doing a cold outreach campaign or presenting in a face-to-face meeting, your sales deck is what makes your product real and relatable. Think of it as a visual story that outlines your product's key features, the problems it solves, and the value it delivers.

Your sales deck should be designed to do one thing: communicate value quickly and effectively. Prospects don't have time to sift through paragraphs of text. Instead, focus on the pain points your product solves, and then clearly show how your features address those pain points. Use high-quality visuals to emphasize these solutions, with each feature paired with a concise explanation of its benefits.

For example, in the early stages of EZOS, I found that the sales deck became my secret weapon. It wasn't enough to tell people what the platform did; I needed a way to visually demonstrate how EZOS could streamline their operations. The sales deck allowed me to showcase features in an engaging format, with visuals that made it easy for prospects to connect the dots between their problems and my solutions.

One effective tip is to integrate a QR code into your deck. This small but powerful addition can significantly increase engagement by making it easier for your target audience to get in touch with you or schedule a demo. By simply scanning the code, they can be taken to your calendar or a dedicated landing page. The easier you make it for prospects to connect with you, the better your chances of moving them down the sales funnel.

The key to a strong sales deck is its flexibility. Like your product, your deck should evolve based on feedback and the changing needs of your audience. As you learn more about what resonates with different customer segments, be prepared to make adjustments. For example, adding customer testimonials or case studies can bolster your credibility, while refining the call to action can help clarify the next steps for prospects.

If the sales deck is about showcasing your product's features and benefits, the investor pitch deck is about selling the vision of your company. It's not just about the product—it's about your team, your market, and your potential for growth. This deck should convince investors that you have the solution to a significant problem, that you understand the market, and that you're the right team to execute the vision.

Investors are looking for compelling reasons to believe in your company. This begins with a strong title slide that includes your company name, logo, and a succinct tagline that captures the essence of your mission. The goal is to intrigue the audience from the start. Your company summary slide should provide a high-level overview of your business—something that captures their attention immediately. If you have traction—whether that's revenue growth, user adoption, or strategic partnerships—make sure to showcase that here.

Next, clearly outline the problem you are solving. What market gap or inefficiency are you addressing? This should be followed by a solution slide, where you explain how your product uniquely solves this problem. Investors want to know why your solution stands out, so be sure to focus on your competitive advantage and the unique value you bring to the market.

The market size slide is critical. Investors want to understand the opportunity for growth. Presenting a clear analysis of your total addressable market (TAM), serviceable addressable market (SAM), and your initial target market demonstrates that you've done your homework and have a strategic approach to scaling.

Your business model should answer the fundamental question: how will you make money? Whether it's through subscription-based services, a freemium model, or enterprise contracts, your business model must show a path to profitability. Additionally, the go-to-market strategy slide should outline how you plan to acquire customers and scale your business, whether through digital marketing, partnerships, or direct sales.

One slide that often trips up founders is the competition slide. It's essential to acknowledge your competitors and highlight how your approach or technology gives you an edge. Investors want to know you've done your research, and they want to understand why your solution is different and better.

The ask slide is where you outline how much funding you are seeking and what you plan to do with it. Be clear about how this investment will help you achieve specific milestones, such as product development, marketing, or expanding your team. The use of funds slide should break down the allocation of the investment—whether it's 40 percent toward development, 30 percent toward marketing, or 20 percent toward hiring.

Perhaps the most crucial slide of all is the "Why You, Why Now" slide. This is your opportunity to explain why your company is the right one to capitalize on this moment in the market. You need to communicate why you're the team to make it happen and why now is the perfect time to invest in your vision.

Both your sales deck and investor deck are living documents. They should grow and evolve as your company scales, your product improves, and your market knowledge deepens. Don't be afraid to iterate and experiment. As you pitch more prospects and investors, you'll gain invaluable feedback that can help refine your messaging, visuals, and structure.

For instance, I've changed both my sales and investor decks multiple times throughout my journey with EZOS. Each iteration made the decks sharper, more concise, and more effective. Being open to this feedback loop is essential for success. Your decks will never be "done"— they will continuously evolve alongside your business.

Success doesn't always come from landing the first investor or customer; it comes from resilience and persistence. As you refine your decks, you'll become more confident in your pitch, and that confidence will resonate with both customers and investors alike.

Lastly, it's not just what's in your deck—it's how you present it. Visual design matters. Keep your slides clean and professional, with a consistent color scheme that reflects your brand. High-quality visuals, graphs, and infographics can make complex information easier to digest. Avoid clutter and text-heavy slides. Instead, aim for bullet points, concise statements, and plenty of white space.

Equally important is practicing your delivery. Knowing your deck inside and out is crucial, especially for investor pitches. Practice until you can present without relying heavily on the slides. This not only ensures a smoother delivery but also allows you to engage with your audience more effectively.

Crafting compelling sales and investor pitch decks is both an art and a science. While your sales deck should focus on delivering clear value to customers, your investor deck must communicate the bigger picture—the vision, the opportunity, and the potential for exponential growth. By continually refining these tools, staying open to feedback, and presenting your message with clarity and confidence, you will set your start-up on a path toward success.

CHAPTER 15

Preparing for Investor Meetings

I used to think that chasing the dream of playing in the NFL would be the toughest challenge I'd ever face, filled with more obstacles than anything I could encounter in the business world. But that was before I started raising capital for EZOS. Raising capital is not for the faint of heart; it's a daunting task that demands your full attention as a CEO. I'm the kind of person who likes to do everything myself, and I've never been comfortable asking for help, especially when it feels like asking for money. So stepping into the world of venture capital and fundraising felt completely out of my element. But I had to shift my mindset and understand that raising capital isn't about asking to be saved; it's about taking the next step in my business journey and finding the right partners—Venture Capitalists (VCs) or any investors who want to join me on this adventure. I've made plenty of mistakes along the way, bumped my head more times than I can count, and learned some hard lessons, but I hope my experiences can help guide you through yours.

My initial approach to fundraising was to rely on sales to validate and grow the business. Every time I received negative feedback from investors, I would return my focus to sales, building the business so that they couldn't provide the same critiques again. Over time, I realized that investors have a set of standard responses: "it's too early," "not enough traction," "not a fit for me," and so on. These responses can be frustrating, but they are a part of the process no matter how big your company gets. The key lesson I learned is that raising capital must be treated as a full-time job. It wasn't my full-time job initially, but if you want to be successful, you must dedicate yourself fully to the task.

One of my biggest mistakes was pitching to only 25 to 30 investors, gathering their feedback, and then retreating to focus on sales. When my business grew and I went back out to raise funds again, I found myself starting from scratch. I hadn't kept those initial investors updated on my progress, so each time I engaged, I had to retell the entire story. This was a significant misstep. As I improved my approach to raising capital, I realized the importance of maintaining ongoing relationships with potential investors. After pitching, add them on LinkedIn and include them in a regular investor update list. Whether you choose to update them monthly or quarterly—my preference is quarterly—keeping them informed about your progress is crucial.

When preparing to pitch to investors, spend 15 to 30 minutes researching the person and the fund you're pitching to. Ensure that you understand their investment criteria and tailor your offering to align with their interests. Remember, investors want to see a potential $100\,x$ return on their investment. Convincing them of your ability to deliver that kind of return is key to getting funded. Your vision needs to be BIG, and you need to have a clear strategy to achieve it. This vision can evolve over time, but initially, set yourself up with the best chance to succeed and don't shortchange your aspirations.

Crafting your pitch involves creating a compelling narrative. You need to articulate your vision clearly and concisely, demonstrating how your product or service solves a significant problem in a large market. Your pitch should cover all the critical aspects: the problem, your solution, the market opportunity, your business model, your traction, and your team. Investors want to see that you have thought through every aspect of your business and that you have a plan for scaling and achieving substantial growth.

Answering investor questions is an art. Be prepared for a range of questions, from detailed inquiries about your financial projections to broader questions about your market strategy. Transparency is key—if you don't know the answer to a question, admit it and commit to following up later with the correct information. Investors appreciate honesty and a willingness to find the right answers. They also want to see how you handle pressure and challenges, so remain calm and composed, demonstrating your adaptability and resourcefulness.

Negotiating terms and agreements can be one of the most challenging parts of the fundraising process. It's important to understand the terms being offered and how they will affect your company. Key terms to focus on include valuation, equity dilution, liquidation preferences, and control rights. Having a lawyer experienced in venture capital can be beneficial in navigating these discussions. Remember, the goal is to secure the funding you need while retaining enough control and ownership to drive your vision forward. Be prepared to negotiate and stand firm on terms that are crucial for your company's long-term success.

Throughout my journey with EZOS, I learned that pitching for volume is essential. Raising capital successfully means speaking to hundreds of investors at each round and following up with all of them consistently. This approach increases your chances of finding a group that believes in your vision and is willing to support you. By keeping investors updated with regular progress reports, you maintain their interest and demonstrate your ongoing commitment and growth.

When it comes to crafting your pitch, think of it as telling a story. Start with the problem you are addressing and why it's significant. Use real-world examples and data to illustrate the pain points your target market faces. Then, introduce your solution, highlighting its unique features and benefits. Explain how your product or service addresses the problem in a way that competitors do not. Use visuals and demonstrations if possible to make your points more compelling.

Your market opportunity slide should showcase the size and growth potential of your market. Use credible sources and data to back up your claims. Investors want to know that there is a large and growing market for your product. Next, outline your business model, explaining how you plan to make money. Be clear about your revenue streams, pricing strategy, and sales approach. Showing that you have a well-thought-out plan for generating revenue is crucial.

Traction is another critical element of your pitch. Demonstrate any progress you have made so far, such as user growth, revenue milestones, partnerships, or pilot programs. Traction provides evidence that your business is gaining momentum and that there is demand for your product. Highlighting key metrics and milestones shows investors that your business is on the right track.

The team slide is where you showcase the people behind the business. Highlight the expertise and experience of your founding team and key hires. Investors invest in people as much as they do in ideas, so it's important to demonstrate that you have a capable and committed team. Include brief bios and relevant achievements to build confidence in your team's ability to execute the business plan.

The "Why You, Why Now" slide is your chance to drive home the urgency and uniqueness of your opportunity. Explain why now is the perfect time for your company to succeed. Highlight any market trends, technological advancements, or regulatory changes that make your solution particularly timely. Emphasize why you and your team are uniquely positioned to capture this opportunity and achieve success.

Visual design is a critical aspect of both sales and investor pitch decks. A clean, professional design can make your presentation more engaging and easier to follow. Use high-quality visuals to support your points and keep your slides uncluttered. Avoid using too much text; instead, use bullet points and short paragraphs to make your content easily digestible. Practice delivering your pitch with the deck to ensure it flows well and that you can speak confidently about each slide. This preparation will help you make a strong impression during presentations.

In summary, preparing for investor meetings involves meticulous preparation, understanding your audience, and continuous follow-up. By pitching to a large volume of investors, keeping them updated, and being clear about your big vision and strategy, you increase your chances of securing the funding you need. My journey with EZOS has taught me the importance of perseverance and adaptability in the fundraising process. With the right approach, you can navigate the complexities of investor meetings and set your company on the path to success. Remember, raising capital is a marathon, not a sprint. Stay focused, keep refining your pitch, and maintain your belief in your vision. Your persistence and dedication will ultimately pay off.

CHAPTER 16

Navigating Legal and Regulatory Challenges

Navigating legal and regulatory challenges is a fundamental aspect of running a tech company. While many in the tech ecosystem suggest hiring legal support to handle contracts, privacy terms, terms and conditions, and other legal matters, I believe it's possible to manage many of these issues through diligent research and self-education. Hiring a lawyer can be expensive, and in the early stages, your budget might be better spent elsewhere. However, there are critical areas where you must ensure legal compliance to protect your company and stakeholders.

Compliance and governance are vital for tech companies. Setting up the right corporate governance structures, maintaining accurate financial records, and ensuring compliance with local, state, and federal laws can help avoid legal issues and build trust with investors, customers, and partners. Proper governance involves establishing a board of directors or advisers who can provide guidance and oversight as your company grows. These individuals can help you navigate complex legal and regulatory landscapes and make informed decisions that benefit your company in the long run.

Regularly reviewing your compliance status and conducting audits can help identify and address potential issues before they become significant problems. This proactive approach can save your company from costly legal battles and ensure that you are always operating within the boundaries of the law. It also demonstrates to investors and partners that you take compliance seriously, which can enhance your credibility and attractiveness as a business partner.

When it comes to submitting your app to app stores, having well-drafted terms and conditions and privacy policies is necessary.

These documents outline the rules for using your app and how you handle user data. They protect your company from legal disputes and ensure that users understand their rights and obligations. App stores such as Google Play and the Apple App Store have specific requirements for these documents, and failure to comply can result in your app being rejected. Drafting clear and concise terms and conditions and privacy policies that comply with app store guidelines is essential. These documents should be easily accessible to users, and any updates should be communicated clearly.

While you can find templates and resources online to help draft these documents, it's essential to customize them to fit your specific business needs. This might involve spending time researching best practices and legal requirements relevant to your industry and target market. For critical contracts, such as those related to hires and cofounders, consulting with a legal professional can be beneficial to ensure that all aspects are covered. Clear equity distribution terms, for example, are crucial in preventing disputes and misunderstandings down the line. Make sure everyone understands how their equity will vest and under what conditions, which can help maintain harmony within your founding team.

In my experience, navigating these legal and regulatory challenges requires diligence and attention to detail. When I started EZOS, I spent considerable time researching the legal requirements and drafting the necessary documents. While it was time-consuming, it saved significant costs and ensured that I was well-prepared to handle any legal issues that arose. By focusing on compliance, data privacy, and clear contractual agreements, you can build a solid legal foundation for your tech company.

Additionally, it's important to stay updated on any changes in the legal landscape that could affect your business. Laws and regulations are constantly evolving, especially in the tech industry. Subscribing to industry newsletters, joining professional organizations, and attending relevant conferences can help you stay informed about new developments. This proactive approach ensures that you are always prepared to adapt to new legal requirements and maintain compliance.

Another key aspect of legal compliance is protecting your intellectual property (IP). Your IP is one of your most valuable assets, and safeguarding it should be a top priority. This includes trademarks, patents, copyrights, and trade secrets. Understanding the different types of IP protection and how to apply for them can prevent others from copying or infringing on your ideas and products. Working with an IP attorney can be beneficial in this area, as they can guide you through the process of securing the necessary protections and defending your IP rights if needed.

It's also crucial to have proper employment contracts and agreements in place. These documents should clearly outline the terms of employment, including roles and responsibilities, compensations, benefits, and termination conditions. For cofounders, it's important to have a founder's agreement that details equity distribution, decision-making processes, and conflict resolution mechanisms. These agreements can prevent misunderstandings and disputes, ensuring that everyone is on the same page from the start.

In conclusion, navigating legal and regulatory challenges is a crucial step in running a successful tech company. By understanding security regulations, ensuring compliance and governance, and drafting clear terms and conditions and privacy policies, you can protect your business and build trust with your stakeholders. My journey with EZOS has shown me the importance of being proactive and thorough in addressing these legal aspects. I encourage all entrepreneurs to take these steps seriously to safeguard their companies' future. While it may seem daunting, investing time and effort into legal compliance can save you from significant headaches and costs down the line. Remember, a solid legal foundation is not just about avoiding trouble; it's about building a company that is trusted, respected, and positioned for long-term success.

CHAPTER 17

Forming Your Business Entity

If you are planning to raise capital for your business, incorporating your company is a crucial step. Most tech companies choose to become Delaware C-corporations (C-corps) due to the tax benefits and the fact that this structure is widely understood and accepted by venture capitalists. My journey started differently. I initially created an LLC in Kentucky, as I had done with my previous small business, Helping Hands. However, when I began raising capital, I quickly discovered that investors were hesitant to invest in an LLC. To address this, I created a Kentucky C-corp as the parent company to the LLC and raised funds through the parent company. This experience taught me that early mistakes in your business structure can be rectified, so there's no need to panic.

Choosing the right business entity is a critical decision that depends on your business goals and plans for raising capital. An LLC can be an excellent choice for small businesses due to its simplicity and flexibility. LLCs provide limited liability protection to their owners, meaning that personal assets are generally protected from business debts and liabilities. Additionally, LLCs offer pass-through taxation, where business income is reported on the owners' personal tax returns, avoiding the double taxation faced by C-corps. However, if you plan to raise significant capital and work with venture capitalists, a C-corp is typically the preferred structure. C-corps offer advantages such as easier transfer of ownership, the ability to issue multiple classes of stock, and no restrictions on the number of shareholders. These features make C-corps more attractive to investors.

Delaware is often the state of choice for incorporation due to its favorable business laws and tax benefits. Delaware has a well-established body of corporate law that provides clarity and predictability for businesses. Additionally, Delaware's tax structure is advantageous, with no state corporate income tax for companies that do not conduct business within the state. These benefits make Delaware an appealing choice for many tech start-ups.

When you are ready to legally register your business, you can do so through the Secretary of State's office in the state where you are incorporating. This process typically involves filing a Certificate of Incorporation (for C-corps) or Articles of Organization (for LLCs), paying the required fees, and drafting bylaws or an operating agreement to govern the company's operations. Many entrepreneurs also use online resources and services to simplify the process of forming business entities. These services can help you file the necessary paperwork, create bylaws, and obtain an Employer Identification Number (EIN) from the Internal Revenue Service (IRS) which is a government agency responsible for collecting taxes and enforcing tax laws. While these services can be convenient, it's still important to understand the requirements and regulations in your specific state.

One crucial aspect of forming your business entity is ensuring that your legal documents accurately reflect the ownership structure and equity distribution among founders and early employees. This includes drafting founder agreements that outline the equity split, vesting schedules, and roles and responsibilities. Vesting schedules are particularly important as they ensure that founders earn their equity over time, typically over a four-year period with a one-year cliff. This structure helps retain key personnel and aligns their interests with the long-term success of the company.

My advice is not to feel rushed to form your business entity. The most important time to have your business officially formed is when you start taking in money, either from customers or investors. If you haven't reached that point yet, focus on developing your product and building your customer base first. Once you are ready to take in money, you can set up your company officially. This approach allows you to avoid unnecessary administrative costs and complexities early on and ensures that your business structure aligns with your operational needs and growth plans.

In my case, the initial setup as an LLC was a learning experience. When I needed to raise capital, transitioning to a C-corp structure allowed me to align with investor expectations and facilitate funding. This flexibility in structuring your business is crucial. You can always adapt and modify your business entity as your needs evolve. For example, you might start as an LLC to take advantage of its simplicity and pass-through taxation, then convert to a C-corp when you are ready to raise institutional capital.

In addition to the structure and incorporation process, it's essential to consider the ongoing compliance and governance requirements for your business entity. C-corps, in particular, have more stringent regulatory requirements, including holding regular board and shareholder meetings, maintaining detailed corporate records, and filing annual reports with the state. Staying compliant with these requirements is vital to maintaining your corporation's good standing and protecting your limited liability status.

Forming your business entity is a foundational step in building your tech company. By choosing the right structure, whether it's an LLC, C-corp, or another entity, you set the stage for future growth and investment. Understanding the legal requirements and taking the time to set up your business correctly will save you headaches down the road. My journey with EZOS taught me the importance of this step and how crucial it is to get it right when you're ready to scale and attract investment.

In conclusion, forming your business entity involves careful consideration of your long-term goals and immediate needs. Whether you choose an LLC for its simplicity or a C-corp for its investor-friendly structure, the key is to ensure that your business is legally sound and ready for growth. By taking the time to understand your options and making informed decisions, you can build a solid foundation for your tech company's success. This foundation will not only facilitate capital raising but also provide the legal and structural framework necessary to support your business as it grows and evolves.

CHAPTER 18

Building Your Founding Team

When I first embarked on my tech journey, I was a one-man show, handling every aspect of the start-up process myself. I drew the wireframes, found a company to build the app, and managed all the initial stages of development. During this time, I realized the importance of having a partner who could complement my knowledge and expertise. This realization led me to my cofounder, whom I met at a mutual job site where both he and my company, Helping Hands, were working. We started talking, and I shared my tech idea with him. We exchanged contact information, and as I got to know him better, it became clear that he would make a great cofounder.

With his extensive experience as a property manager and head facilities person, he essentially represented my ICP. If he were still working those jobs, we would be selling directly to him. His deep understanding of the industry allowed him to speak the language of our target customers during demos, which proved invaluable. He handles sales demos, account management, implementation, and training for our customers, and oversees his account manager team as our company COO. It took several meetings to convince him to partner up, offering a combination of equity and a salary that worked for both parties.

As the CEO, especially in the early stages, you may need to pay a salary and offer equity to your first team members. One of the biggest advantages of having your small business still operating while building your tech company is the ability to use funds from your small business to support the salaries of early team members for your tech company. This financial flexibility allows you to recruit talent even when your tech company can't afford the salaries on its own. Once the tech company becomes financially stable, you can transfer these expenses to the tech company's books.

During our first year with EZOS, we did not have a technical cofounder. We outsourced all development work, which led to challenges, particularly with the time required to fix bugs, which wasn't ideal for our customers. Therefore, our next critical hire was a technical cofounder who could build and manage our entire system. We found this cofounder by talking to teachers at local schools, identifying their best students, interviewing them, and pitching the opportunity to join a fast-growing tech company. By the second year, our founding team consisted of myself as CEO, my first cofounder as COO, and our third cofounder as CTO.

In my experience, the most crucial roles for a founding team are a technical founder and a sales founder. The more technical expertise you have on your founding team, the better equipped you are to handle the product development and technical challenges that arise. Each founder should have equity in the company, which should be earned on a vesting schedule of three to four years with a one-year cliff. This vesting and cliff schedule is essential because it provides a year to assess whether the team fit is right. If it isn't, changes can be made without losing equity. The vesting schedule ensures a long-term commitment of three to four years, during which everyone is fully invested in seeing the business succeed.

Identifying key team roles is vital in building a solid foundation for your company. The CEO typically handles the overall vision, strategy, and operations, while the COO focuses on the day-to-day management and execution of the business plan. The CTO is responsible for the technical direction and development of the product. Having a diverse set of skills and expertise within the founding team ensures that all critical aspects of the business are covered and managed effectively.

Equity distribution strategies should be carefully considered and clearly communicated among the founding team. It's crucial to discuss and agree on how equity will be allocated based on each founder's role, contribution, and commitment to the company. This discussion should include the vesting schedule and cliff to ensure that everyone understands the terms and is aligned with the company's long-term goals.

Hiring talent with equity is a powerful tool for attracting and retaining top talent, especially when the company is in its early stages and may not have the resources to offer competitive salaries. By offering equity, you can provide an incentive for team members to invest in the company's success and align their interests with those of the company. This approach not only helps in building a strong, committed team but also fosters a sense of ownership and responsibility among team members.

Building your founding team is a crucial step in establishing your tech company. By identifying key roles, developing equity distribution strategies, and leveraging equity to attract talent, you can create a strong foundation for your company's growth and success. My journey with EZOS has taught me the importance of having a complementary team, clear agreements, and a shared commitment to the company's vision. With the right team in place, you can navigate the challenges of building a tech company and achieve your entrepreneurial goals.

The process of finding and convincing a cofounder requires persistence and strategic thinking. During my initial conversations with potential cofounders, I focused on understanding their career goals, expertise, and how they could contribute to the company. It's essential to find someone who shares your vision and has the skills you lack. For instance, my cofounder's experience in property management and facilities made him an invaluable asset in understanding our target market's needs and speaking their language.

Another critical aspect of building your founding team is ensuring that everyone is aligned with the company's mission and values. This alignment fosters a cohesive team environment where everyone is working toward the same goals. It's important to have open and honest conversations about the company's direction, challenges, and opportunities. These discussions help build trust and ensure that all team members are committed to the company's success.

As you grow your team, consider the long-term needs of your company. While the initial focus may be on technical and sales roles, other functions such as marketing, finance, and customer support will become important as your company scales. Planning for these future hires and understanding when to bring them on board is crucial for sustained growth. Each new hire should bring skills and expertise that complement the existing team and help fill gaps in the company's capabilities.

In addition to internal hires, building a network of advisers and mentors can provide valuable guidance and support. Advisers can offer insights based on their experience, help you navigate challenges, and provide introductions to potential investors, partners, and customers. Having a diverse group of advisers with expertise in different areas can significantly enhance your company's strategic decision making.

The process of building your founding team and expanding your company's capabilities is ongoing. As your company grows and evolves, so will your team's needs. Regularly reassess your team structure and make adjustments as necessary to ensure that you have the right people in the right roles. This adaptability is crucial for responding to market changes, scaling your operations, and achieving your company's long-term vision.

In conclusion, building your founding team involves careful planning, strategic thinking, and a commitment to finding the right people who share your vision and values. By identifying key roles, developing equity distribution strategies, and leveraging equity to attract top talent, you can create a strong foundation for your tech company's growth and success. My journey with EZOS has reinforced the importance of having a complementary team, clear agreements, and a shared commitment to the company's vision. With the right team in place, you can navigate the challenges of building a tech company and achieve your entrepreneurial goals.

PART 5

Launching and Sustaining Your Tech Company

CHAPTER 19

Building a Sustainable Team and Leading Through Change

In football, there's a saying that's often repeated by coaches and players alike: "It's not the X's and O's, but the Jimmys and the Joes that make the difference." This phrase emphasizes that while strategy and playbooks are critical, it's the players—the individuals who execute those strategies—who ultimately determine the outcome of the game. You can have the most sophisticated playbook, the most innovative strategies, and the most advanced training techniques, but if you don't have the right players on the field, your chances of success are slim. The same principle applies in the business world, especially in the fast-paced, ever-changing tech industry. Your business can have the most cutting-edge technology, the best software, and the most brilliant ideas, but without a strong team of dedicated, talented individuals, those assets won't be enough to carry you to victory.

The Importance of the Right Team

When I first transitioned from the NFL to entrepreneurship, I quickly realized that building a business is a lot like building a football team. In both arenas, success hinges on having the right people in the right positions. You need individuals who not only have the skills to execute the playbook but who also share a common vision and are committed to working together toward a shared goal.

In football, every player has a specific role to play, whether it's the quarterback, who must make split-second decisions under pressure, or the offensive lineman, who must protect the quarterback at all costs. Each role is crucial, and the team's success depends on how well each player performs their role and how well they work together as a unit. Similarly, in a tech company, you need a diverse team with a wide range of skills and expertise. You need software developers who can build and maintain your product, marketers who can communicate its value to the world, salespeople who can close deals, and customer support teams who can ensure your users are satisfied.

But having the right skills isn't enough. Just as in football, where a team's chemistry and cohesion can make or break its performance, in business, the culture and dynamics of your team are critical. You need people who are not only skilled but also aligned with your company's values and mission. They need to be able to collaborate effectively, communicate openly, and trust one another. Without these qualities, even the most talented individuals can struggle to work together effectively, leading to missed opportunities and failed projects.

Recruiting the "Jimmys and the Joes"

Recruiting the right team members is one of the most important tasks you'll undertake as a leader. In football, coaches spend countless hours scouting players, analyzing their performance, and assessing how they'll fit into the team's overall strategy. In business, the recruitment process should be just as rigorous. It's not just about filling positions; it's about finding individuals who will contribute to the long-term success of your company.

When I was building my team at EZOS, I looked for people who not only had the technical skills we needed but who also shared my passion for innovation and my commitment to excellence. I wanted people who were not just looking for a job but who were excited about the opportunity to build something new and make a real impact. This meant taking the time to get to know candidates beyond their resumes, understanding their motivations, and assessing how they would fit into our company culture.

It's also important to recognize that diversity is a key strength in any team. In football, a team of players who all have the same strengths and weaknesses will struggle against a more balanced team. The same is true in business. A diverse team brings a range of perspectives, experiences, and ideas, which can lead to more innovative solutions and better decision making. This diversity should not only be in terms of skills and expertise but also in terms of background, gender, race, and culture. A team that reflects a wide range of viewpoints is better equipped to understand and meet the needs of a diverse customer base.

Creating a Culture of Collaboration

Once you've assembled your team, the next challenge is to create a culture where collaboration and innovation can thrive. In football, the best teams are those where players trust each other, communicate openly, and are willing to put the team's success above their own individual achievements. The same principles apply in business.

At EZOS, we made it a priority to foster a culture of open communication and mutual respect. We encouraged team members to share their ideas, ask questions, and challenge assumptions. This wasn't just about making everyone feel included; it was about recognizing that the best ideas often come from unexpected places. By creating an environment where everyone felt comfortable contributing, we were able to tap into the full range of our team's talents and creativity.

One of the ways we encouraged collaboration was through regular team meetings and brainstorming sessions. These weren't just status updates; they were opportunities for everyone to weigh in on the challenges we were facing and to propose solutions. We found that by involving the whole team in problem-solving, we were able to come up with more creative and effective solutions than we would have if decisions were made by a few people at the top.

Leading Through Change

The tech industry is constantly evolving, and as a leader, you need to be able to guide your team through change. Just as a football coach needs to adapt the team's strategy based on the opponent and the conditions on game day, a business leader needs to be able to pivot in response to changes in the market, new technological developments, and shifting customer needs.

One of the most significant challenges I faced as a leader was knowing when to stick with a strategy and when to pivot. When we first launched EZOS, we were focused on solving specific pain points in property management. However, as we grew and the market evolved, it became clear that we needed to expand our offerings to stay competitive. This required a strategic pivot, which meant not only shifting our product focus but also leading our team through the transition. This was not an easy process, but by communicating clearly and involving the team in decision making, we were able to navigate the change successfully.

Leading through change requires more than just making decisions at the top. It requires involving your team in the process, getting their buy-in, and helping them understand the reasons behind the changes. This is particularly important in a tech company, where change is often fast-paced and can be unsettling for team members. By keeping the lines of communication open and providing support and guidance, you can help your team navigate change more effectively.

Empowering Your Team

Empowerment is another crucial aspect of leadership. Your team needs to feel empowered to make decisions and take ownership of their work. This not only boosts their confidence but also leads to better outcomes for the company. Empowerment is about trust. You need to trust that your team members have the skills and knowledge to do their jobs effectively, and they need to trust that you will support them in their decisions.

At EZOS, we empower our team members by giving them autonomy over their projects. This means setting clear expectations and providing the necessary resources, but allowing them the freedom to approach the task in their way. This approach has led to increased innovation and efficiency, as team members feel more invested in the success of their projects.

Empowerment also means recognizing and rewarding achievements. In football, players who make significant contributions are often recognized through awards or increased playing time. In business, it's important to celebrate successes, whether it's through formal recognition programs or simply acknowledging a job well done. This not only boosts morale but also reinforces the behaviors and attitudes that contribute to the company's success.

Resilience: The Key to Long-Term Success

Resilience is a quality that every entrepreneur and leader must possess. The road to success is rarely smooth, and there will be setbacks along the way. How you respond to these challenges will determine the future of your company. Resilience is not just about bouncing back from failures; it's about learning from them and coming back stronger.

In the early days of EZOS, we faced numerous challenges, from technical issues to market resistance. There were times when it felt like everything was going wrong, but giving up was never an option. Instead, we used these challenges as learning opportunities. Each setback taught us something new and helped us refine our approach. This resilience is what has kept EZOS growing and evolving, even in the face of adversity.

Resilience is also about maintaining your focus and determination, even when things get tough. Just as in football, where the best teams are often the ones that can stay focused and keep pushing through the toughest games, in business, the most successful companies are those that can stay the course, even in the face of adversity. This requires a strong sense of purpose, a clear vision, and the ability to stay motivated, even when the odds are against you.

Conclusion: The Power of a Strong Team

In conclusion, building a strong team and leading with vision, collaboration, and resilience are critical to the success of any tech company. Your team is your most valuable asset, and as a leader, it's your responsibility to nurture and guide them. The tech industry is dynamic and challenging, but with the right team and strong leadership, there's no limit to what you can achieve.

Remember, leadership is not about having all the answers; it's about creating an environment where your team can thrive and work together toward a common goal. As you build your tech company, focus on assembling a team that shares your vision, creating a culture of collaboration, and leading with resilience and adaptability. These qualities will set your company on the path to success, no matter what challenges come your way.

Just as in football, where the Jimmys and the Joes ultimately determine the outcome of the game, in business, it's the people on your team who will make the difference. Invest in them, empower them, and lead them through the inevitable changes and challenges, and they will help you achieve your goals and take your company to new heights.

CHAPTER 20

Launching and Sustaining Your Tech Company

With everything in place, you are prepared to officially launch your tech company alongside your small business. This is an exhilarating and pivotal moment in your entrepreneurial journey, one that requires a blend of vision, strategy, and relentless execution. As you embark on this path, my final advice is to focus intensely on customer feedback and retention. Listening to your customers throughout the sales cycle and ensuring that their needs are met is crucial, especially in the early stages when your company's foundation is being laid. Customer-centricity isn't just a buzzword; it's the core of sustainable growth. While customizations may become less feasible as you scale, initially tailoring your product to meet specific customer needs can help you secure those first crucial contracts. Building your company around your customers' needs and refining your product based on their feedback is a powerful strategy to ensure your product resonates with the market.

Once your customers start using your product, actively seek their feedback and be prepared to make necessary adjustments. Use their testimonials and success stories as powerful tools to win over new prospects. If you consistently have satisfied customers, you will likely have a thriving business that can withstand market fluctuations. At EZOS, we have always prioritized our customers, building our brand and loyalty around exceptional customer support and making our customers feel like integral parts of our company as we grow. This approach has not only driven our success but also fostered a sense of community and shared purpose.

Preparing for the launch of your tech company requires meticulous planning and execution. Consider starting with a soft launch to test your product in a real-world environment with a limited number of users. This approach allows you to identify and address any issues before the official launch, mitigating risks and ensuring a smoother rollout. Use this period to gather valuable feedback, make necessary improvements, and build initial traction. Word-of-mouth marketing, often generated during a soft launch, can be one of the most powerful drivers of early adoption.

When it comes time for the official launch, develop a comprehensive strategy that includes marketing, PR, and sales efforts. Utilize multiple channels to reach your target audience, such as social media, email marketing, industry events, and strategic partnerships. Creating excitement around your launch is essential; consider offering promotions, hosting webinars, or providing exclusive access to early adopters. Ensure that your team is fully prepared to handle an influx of new users and provide exceptional customer support. The first impression you make during your launch can set the tone for your company's future success.

Gathering and analyzing user feedback postlaunch is essential for continuous improvement and customer satisfaction. Implement mechanisms for collecting feedback, such as surveys, user interviews, and in-app feedback forms. Regularly review this feedback to identify common themes and areas for improvement. Prioritize critical issues and work closely with your development team to address them promptly. Engaging with your customers and demonstrating that you value their input builds trust, loyalty, and a strong brand reputation.

Use customer feedback not only to improve your product but also to inform your sales and marketing strategies. Highlight positive feedback and success stories in your marketing materials to attract new customers. Demonstrating that you listen to and act on customer feedback can set you apart from competitors, enhancing your reputation and fostering long-term relationships with your customers.

Planning for future growth involves setting clear goals and developing a strategic roadmap to achieve them. Identify KPIs to measure your progress and adjust your strategies as needed. Continuously evaluate your market position, competition, and industry trends to stay ahead of the curve. As your company grows, invest in scaling your operations, expanding your team, and enhancing your product offerings to meet the evolving needs of your customers.

Consider long-term strategies for customer retention, such as developing loyalty programs, offering advanced features, and providing ongoing support and training. Retaining existing customers is often more cost-effective than acquiring new ones, and loyal customers can become advocates for your brand, driving organic growth and reducing customer acquisition costs.

As you launch and sustain your tech company, it's important to recognize the value of building strong relationships with your customers. Personalize your interactions, provide exceptional support, and go the extra mile to ensure their satisfaction. By fostering a customer-centric culture, you create an environment where customers feel valued and are more likely to remain loyal to your brand. This loyalty is a key driver of long-term success, especially in an increasingly competitive market.

One of the most effective ways to sustain your tech company is by continually innovating and improving your product. Stay ahead of the competition by keeping up with industry trends and technological advancements. Regularly update your product with new features and improvements based on customer feedback and market demands. This not only enhances the user experience but also demonstrates your commitment to providing the best possible solution for your customers, helping you maintain a competitive edge.

Additionally, focus on building a strong company culture that attracts and retains top talent. Your team plays a crucial role in the success of your tech company, so invest in their development and well-being. Create a positive work environment where employees feel motivated, valued, and inspired to contribute to the company's growth. A dedicated and passionate team will drive innovation, deliver exceptional customer service, and help your company achieve its long-term goals. The culture you cultivate within your company will be reflected in your product, your customer interactions, and ultimately, your success.

As your tech company grows, it's important to establish robust processes and systems to manage your operations effectively. This includes implementing efficient project management tools, automating repetitive tasks, and streamlining workflows. By optimizing your internal processes, you can improve productivity, reduce costs, and ensure that your team can focus on strategic initiatives that drive growth. Efficiency and scalability are crucial as your company expands, allowing you to maintain the quality and integrity of your operations.

Financial management is another critical aspect of sustaining your tech company. Keep a close eye on your cash flow, manage your expenses wisely, and plan for future investments. Seek advice from financial experts or consider hiring a CFO (Chief Finanical Officer) to ensure that your company remains financially healthy and can weather any challenges that may arise. Sound financial management will provide the stability needed to support growth and innovation, enabling you to make strategic decisions with confidence.

Another key factor in sustaining your tech company is building a strong network of mentors, advisers, and industry connections. Surround yourself with experienced professionals who can provide guidance, support, and valuable insights. Join industry associations, attend conferences, and actively participate in relevant communities to expand your network and stay informed about industry trends and opportunities. The relationships you build can provide critical support and open doors to new opportunities as your company grows.

As we come to the end of this book, I hope you feel excited and confident about your journey. Building and sustaining a tech company is no small feat, but with the right strategies, a strong focus on customer satisfaction, and a relentless drive, you can achieve remarkable success. Remember, your customers are your greatest asset. By listening to them, adapting to their needs, and continuously improving your product, you can create a loyal customer base that will support your growth and success.

This book has provided you with the foundational knowledge and practical steps to turn your small business expertise into a thriving tech company. Embrace the challenges, learn from the setbacks, and celebrate the victories. Your journey is just beginning, and the possibilities are endless. With dedication, passion, and the right approach, you can build a tech company that not only stands the test of time but also makes a significant impact in your industry.

Here's to your success and the exciting road ahead. Launch boldly, sustain diligently, and always keep your customers at the heart of your mission. Thank you for allowing me to be a part of your journey. Now, go out there and make your vision a reality.

About the Author

Chase Minnifield is uniquely positioned to write *The Tech Audible: Switch the Play from Small Business to Tech*. His journey from professional athlete to successful entrepreneur is both inspiring and instructive, making him an authority on navigating significant career transitions and leveraging diverse experiences to achieve business success.

Chase began his professional journey as a defensive back for the Washington Redskins. His journey to the NFL allowed him to hone his skills in strategy, leadership, teamwork, and discipline. These skills became invaluable when he transitioned from the football field to the business world. At the age of 25, after his NFL career, Chase founded Helping Hand, LLC, a company providing moving, cleaning, and apartment turnover services for college dormitories and student housing complexes. Today, Helping Hand is one of the largest minority-owned security companies in the United States. Under his leadership, Helping Hand has expanded nationwide, partnering with numerous universities and generating over $15 million in revenue since its inception.

It was during his time with Helping Hand that Chase identified significant pain points in the property management and security industries. These insights led to the creation of his two groundbreaking tech companies: EZOS and Gard Technologies. EZOS, originally named EZTurn, was highlighted on the Forbes 30 Under 30 list in 2019 for its innovation and rapid growth. It was born from Chase's firsthand experiences with inefficiencies in property maintenance and invoicing. This software utilizes AI and ML to automate property maintenance scheduling workflows, envisioning a future where very few staff are needed to run and manage properties. Today, EZOS serves over 300,000 users and has generated millions in revenue, illustrating Chase's ability to transform real-world problems into scalable tech solutions.

Gard Technologies, on the other hand, addresses security and public safety challenges. With products such as Gard, a security ERP software, and GardX, a public safety app for retail and apartment complexes, Gard

Technologies provides safe spaces for guests and tenants. Gard Technologies leverages AI to optimize security operations, from hiring to monitoring, and uses real-time data to enhance public safety. This venture again demonstrates Chase's knack for innovation in spaces where his small business operates.

Chase's journey from sports to tech, combined with his hands-on experience in identifying and solving operational inefficiencies, makes him the ideal author for this book. His story is not just about creating successful businesses but also about resilience, innovation, and the relentless pursuit of excellence. Through *The Tech Audible*, Chase aims to empower other entrepreneurs to pivot from traditional business models to tech-driven solutions, sharing the insights and strategies that have fueled his success.

Chase's educational background includes an MA in Sports Administration from the University of Louisville and a BS in Sociology from the University of Virginia.

Index

www.ingramcontent.com/pod-product-compliance
Lightning Source LLC
Chambersburg PA
CBHW061331220326
41599CB00026B/5130